RUNNING
OFF THE
MAP

RUNNING OFF THE MAP

In Search of Sanity

CHRISTOPHER SPRIGGS

Copyright © 2024 by Christopher Spriggs

All rights reserved. No part of this book may be reproduced or used in any manner without the permission of the copyright owner, except for the use of quotations in a book review.

ISBN: 979-8880382064

Cover design & typesetting by Benita Thompson

First Paperback Edition 2024

To K, MJ & T

"Since my house burned down
I now have a better view
of the rising moon"

Mizuta Masahide
17th century
Japanese
samurai
& poet

CONTENTS

Foreword by John Whittington		xi
Part I:	*Fractures*	1
Part II:	*In Search of Sanity*	27
	Autumn	29
	Loch Rannoch	33
	Winter	49
	The Geminids	53
	Hayling Island	67
	Hope Valley	79
	Spring	90
	Wicken Fen	93
	Jurassic Coast	103
	Cheddar Gorge	115
	Summer	123
	Mourne Way	125
	Mount Snowdon	135
	New Forest	148
	Autumn	159
	Dartmoor	163
	Beachy Head	176
	Gower Peninsula	184
	Winter	192
	Kielder Water	194
Part III:	*A Geography of Hope*	207

FOREWORD

Writing that really meets you, that reaches into the human experience, *your* human experience, is hard to find. You have in your hands a book that truly does this, from the first page to the last.

Christopher writes with depth, integrity and coherence about times in his life, in all of our lives, that seem overwhelming, confusing and final.

It is his account of several challenging years, but it is also yours, ours, the story of universal suffering. He sinks into the depths of the human experience and comes back up with clarity and insight in one sentence after another.

If you are serious about the life-long journey of growth, development and integration at both the human and global scale; if you are committed to connecting more deeply with your essence, your true nature; and if you also want to help and are open to being helped, then this book will take you on a rich journey of insights, emotions and truly useful, fresh awareness.

Allow his story to percolate through your own experience of what it means to be human. Let it touch you, challenge you, elevate you.

Life is challenging and sometimes dark. There is much here to illuminate the way.

John Whittington
Author, "Systemic Coaching & Constellations"

Part I

FRACTURES

"What is most personal, is most universal"

—*Carl Rogers*

Tenby, Wales:

Sliding down the cliff feet first, fingers snatch at tussocks of grass, carving the soil with a signature that won't last. Sea coughs on the rocks a hundred feet below. My heart thuds-thuds-THUDS.

A thought as distinct as a dog bark erupts from within, "Oh god, I am going to die." I register each syllable as if the thought occurs in slow motion. Then another thought, this one yapping and insistent, "But - like this? Really? I am going to die... LIKE THIS??"

Only a few months before this I had considered how I might end my own life given how circumstances had conspired to leave me without a secure home or paid work and ten pence left in a savings account. I didn't imagine my own ending to be quite like this. I thought it would be more, well, dramatic. I feel cheated. "Hang on, this wasn't the plan" I want to say to anyone who will listen. But no one is here. Air freezes in my throat. Fingertips tingle. Sweat bubbles in dots upon my forehead before running onto my eyebrows. I grunt a final breath, hearing it expire.

As a child I dreamed of being Superman. A photograph clings to the fridge door in my flat showing a child version of myself, aged ten, wearing Y-front pants over leggings, a red blanket as a cape around my neck and a big 'S' scribbled on a scrap piece of paper pinned to a skinny chest. But here, gripping the cliff edge, no super powers remain, only a forced acceptance that nothing now matters.

I
exhale
two long
puffs as if
sprinting for
the bus but not
sure if I will make it~~~~~~~~~~~~~~~~~~~

"And how are you feeling about the situation now?" my therapist would often ask me during two years of counselling. I chose John to be my therapist from a notice board of 30 qualified therapists. His eyes were soft and his fees were affordable. When we met I would watch the second hand on the plastic clock above his head arriving at the next mark on its perimeter and marvel at how each second choreographed itself in an elaborate dance: Click-Glide-and-Tremble, Click-Glide-and-Tremble, as if the clock was nervous on my behalf, as if it knew about the cliff edge. My book shelves filled up with titles like "*When Things Fall Apart*"; "*Braving The Wilderness*"; "*Falling Upwards*"; "*The Road Less Travelled*". "Well John", I would say if he were here dangling with me on this cliffside, "I am rather scared actually" and John would have nodded with empathy and concern.

Falling down the cliff was never the plan. Whilst walking alone along the cliff top promontory to find a place to sit and read my book, I attempted to make a short climb to reach the high point and survey the horizon like Sargon of Akkad, the first King of the world. I wanted to get that feeling of "ah, so THIS is the world" and feel my feet upon its zenith. But the cliffside path disappeared just where the land tipped itself toward the sea. Was the path I had walked only in my imagination? "How did I end up like this?" I ask myself, soil clogging my fingernails.

On the other side of the promontory is Tenby South Beach where wind slaps my one-man tent, tugging the ropes and bullying the poles. The fireplace still smoulders from last night, a fireplace built with rocks the size of cannonballs, collected one at a time from the shoreline. Perhaps a curl of smoke inscribes an SOS in the air.

Faces of people with whom I had fallen out hammer in my head. Face, after face, after face, like a crowd of accusers. Amongst them is my own. My backpack is heavy as if crammed with resentment so I can't even shake a fist at myself without plunging to the rocks below. I would wriggle free of its weight to give myself a chance of climbing back up but, as well as it containing a full flask of hot water and a handful of tea bags, there is a paperback copy of Homer's "The Odyssey" within. My favourite bookmark is tucked inside its pages, a leather one quoting Rumi the Sufist poet, *"What you seek is seeking you"*, which is hard to believe right now.

I had reached the point in Homer's tale, over 2500 years old but resonating with my ridiculous calamities, where the heroic Odysseus has been spewed up in some place he didn't plan. "The long-enduring Odysseus must now set out for home" decreed Zeus to his son Hermes, the messenger, "On the journey he shall have neither gods nor men to help him." When Hermes catches up with him Odysseus wasn't hiding in Calypso's cave on the island of Ogygia as he suspected but was "sitting disconsolate on the shore...tormenting himself with tears and sighs and heartache, and looking out across the barren sea with steaming eyes." A failure of super powers. But at least Odysseus had somewhere to sit. Reality has me squirming on a cliff, forcing a clinical separation from all the ideas and entitlements about how I think "my life" should work, as if life can be shrunk to fit the pronouns of personal possession.

Crisis ushers us into the jaws of the present moment, "the only moment we ever have", as mathematician and philosopher Blaise Pascal observed 400 years ago, "yet the one we habitually want to escape." I confess: I want to escape the present moment. Give me somewhere to sit, anywhere, even a room with a plastic clock and a nodding therapist. Click-Glide-and-Tremble. Time keeps searching for an escape, the second hand never stopping, not even to wave goodbye.

My body stops sliding. Fingertips and boot-toes are all that keep me on the earth. The limestone bollard of Caldey Island lighthouse stares back from across the water, turning a blind eye to this small self hanging on for dear life. The peacefulness of the moment is like being filled with ice so at least I am going to die chilled. I must own whatever comes next because nobody is coming to the rescue. There is no Calypso to whisk me into her cave or Father Christmas-like deity who will rend the clouds asunder and set my feet upon a rock. Looking over my shoulder I imagine the sea licking its lips at the prospect of swallowing this body and gulping it down whole. The faces swarm again in my mind, echoes of old conversations and feelings of regret. In this moment there is nothing and no one to believe in. Tears draw lines down my cheeks, congregating in my beard like a funeral party. My legs hang heavy and my fingers hurt like hell. The sun burns my scalp.

That's it then.

I. Am. Done.

I breathe out the longest breath from the deepest place as if into a breathalyser expelling all the hope from within my body until bankrupting the caverns of my lungs and there is nothing but vacancy, lips parting, mouth yawning open like the **O** of a tunnel, a place of simultaneous exit and entry.

Something inside dies.

The fury which fuelled the desire for revenge collapses. It is as if all the self-pity, judgement and the story-in-my-brain evaporates. The realisation that I am about to die is like a toilet being flushed clean of 40-something years of accumulated shit.

And then something comes to life.

Shoulders drop, elbows press into the mud, chest eases against the vertical earth as if a deeper defiance is at work. Nudging my right knee up, only millimetres, I press a denim thigh against something solid. Surges of wanting to be sick rush through my body as each movement births risk, backpack jerking from side to side, metronomic, marking a slow rhythm of ascent. As chances of surviving increase, adrenalin surges, until after an eternity of tiny movements I hurl myself back onto a plateau of long grass. Knees kiss dirt, sore fingers plunge into clumps of candy-pink sea thrift, their pin-cushion flower heads tickling my cheeks. I remain hunched like a dog, arms trembling, waiting to vomit. There is solid ground beneath me. It is the most certain thing I have ever known. For a long while I sob, hot tears erupting from an internal reservoir of fright and gratitude.

Walking back to the tent, I notice through a tunnel of sycamore branches the long golden stretch of South Beach punctuated by the singularity of a tent, my solitary canvas outpost, a black dot perched on a strip of sand like a mislaid full stop. Upon my return the tent fabric ripples in the breeze sounding like applause. The gash across the tent roof, caused by a storm on the first night of camping, has lengthened three inches in my absence and through the open slit the sun has fingered a hole in the casing of the plastic stove, its defences pierced by intense light.

I sit upon the roughened bark of a fallen birch tree, 12 feet long, dragged a quarter of a mile from the other end of the beach when I first arrived. Its fractured branches scraped the sand like animal claws on human skin. Picking at the bark with finger and thumb, I feel the full weight of my body as if I have just landed from space. Therapist John comes to mind again. "You know", John had said to me recently, his hands pressing down on his knees, "sometimes life falls apart. It isn't on the menu or in the plan or whatever. Call it grief, failure, growing up. But slowly, life does come together again. It does." Rain zig-zagged down the counselling room window obeying the laws of gravity. I recall

John, hands clasped together in a gesture of self-reflection, right thumb tapping the top of his left hand as if following some tune hidden inside his brain, or perhaps the rhythm of a story with which I am not yet familiar. I was there, but not there. Hearing but not entirely listening.

John asked whether I had heard of an American poet called Walt Whitman. "The guy who looked like Father Christmas?" I said, acting out a long beard and over-sized belly to undermine the seriousness of the moment. John ignored my impersonation. "When Whitman was in his fifties, he had a stroke which left him half-paralysed so he thought about the meaning of life. 'What makes life worth living? Worth remembering?' Those things we think but rarely say. Anyway, after lots of time in nature Whitman wrote to a friend, 'I easily tire, I am very clumsy' he wrote, 'I cannot walk far; but my spirits are first-rate'. And then Whitman came up with three questions, which I offer you: 'What do you stand for? What are you contributing to others around you? And how will you be remembered?'" If only John were here on the fallen birch gazing out to sea I might have something interesting to say between the Click-Glide-and-Tremble of time.

E.V. Rieu, translator of the version of "The Odyssey" still buried in my backpack, says the hero's pattern is repeated throughout Greek mythology like a message in a stick of rock:

First you must survive your downfall.

Then return home - to yourself.

And then you restore what was lost.

Survive, Return, Restore. It's a short list but it takes time. We want life-stage transitions to take an afternoon, but they take years and in one sense never end, like a constant opening up to life. Sitting on the fractured log I consider for the first time what a gigantic success it is just to survive. Some days to survive is everything. Some days surviving IS the point.

The beach is empty. I look to the east where clouds huddle on the horizon, then reawaken the fire using clumps of dead grass from the base of the sand dunes behind the tent. Flames lick into life and from the throat of the fire smoke rises like new breath.

Brighton, England:

A few days ago I stood next to my Uncle Andrew's coffin, a bamboo oblong perched on a wooden plinth. The crematorium bulged with people from his life: ex-colleagues from three decades working with Exxon Mobil, fellow runners from the Horsham Joggers club to which he belonged, and his peers from the worldwide service organisation, Horsham Lions. Three generations of family sat in a long arc of seats, a chain reaction of tears and hugs passing between us. His journey with motor neurone disease (MND), a terminal illness which in his case continued for just over six years, slowly robbed him of mobility, but never courage.

"*One day to run, one day to push; One day to wave, cheer, feel the rush.*" I stand at the lectern and read the poem I had written the day before our Brighton marathon together in 2013. My hands grip the lectern as if I am still pushing his NHS wheelchair at full tilt along Marine Parade then up past the Royal Pavilion. "*One day to enjoy Brighton's breeze on our skin, hear the crowd wooing us further on, further in.*" I feel again the tempo of our racing as words gather momentum. "*A sound to behold and soak in; absorb all the humanity, the hilarity and hope in.*" I hear my voice, alone, filling a room of mourners, with no uncle in a wheelchair behind which I can hide. No clock against which to race. Every story has its finish line and as I end the poem, the crematorium erupts with applause. There's a cheer and a whistle and a woman I don't know on the front row crying. I turn and look at my uncle's coffin, knowing this moment is our finish line, our silent goodbye. I nod, then walk to my seat.

My cousin Paul followed with a tribute, words weighted with pride as he spoke of his dad's love of Pink Floyd, marathon running (forty-one of them in total) and travels around the world with his wife, Sandra. Afterwards we gathered, family and friends, in an oak-beamed Sussex pub where forgotten Christmas decorations were still left up and an open fire spat sparks. We looked through photograph albums swelling with evidence of my uncle's penchant for fancy dress, as if he had been searching for the finest version of himself. Our last race together was the Surrey half marathon in March 2016. "Leave it all on the road" my uncle said to me before the race start, as Sandra zipped up his raincoat and I pulled a woolly hat over his ears. He wasn't referring to the garments, he meant putting maximum effort into the race. Neither of us said it would be our last race but with his physical strength dialling down, we both knew. Lifting his own cutlery was becoming impossible.

Although the illness didn't entirely take his voice, which happens to 8 out of 10 people with MND, there were more gaps and gasps when he spoke. We finished the race in 1 hour and 43 minutes, a personal best for us for that distance. In the final mile, I pushed his wheelchair with my head down, roaring at the road with all the fury I had about a disease that was dismantling his body from the inside. As with all the wheelchair races together - two marathons, five half marathons plus the 10-mile Great South Run - in the evening my auntie poured Prosecco until the bottle was empty (which didn't take long) and we clinked glasses before planning our next race. After the Surrey half marathon, we drank the fizz but abstained on planning, as if we both knew we had reached the end.

When overwhelmed by grief, people search out places where they can clear their head and get a different view. The sea air often becomes a shared source of comfort. Perhaps this is why I've returned to Brighton. In this morning light, Brighton's Palace Pier looks asleep, its 67,000 light bulbs drooping in rows like unawakened minds:

UUUUUUUUUUUUUUUUUUUUU
UUUUUUUUUUUUUUUUUUUU

Waves crack against the pier's iron legs and beyond sits the black-boned solitary skeleton of West Pier, destroyed by fire in 2003. In my eye-line are the two pier structures: the old one destroyed, the new one dormant. "You put together two things that have not been put together before" writes Julian Barnes in "Levels of Life", writing about the tragic loss of his wife, Pat, "and the world is changed. People may not notice at the time, but that doesn't matter. The world has been changed nonetheless."

Two people, two places, two moments.

Walking from the pier onto the beach, stones slide underfoot. As I remember my uncle's funeral, a herring gull tilts its wings in the wind in front of me, composing itself. It doesn't seem to want to go anywhere, suspended as if under the command of a master puppeteer. Once in Cley next the Sea - an eastern coastline at a different time - I watched dozens of gulls self-correct in strong winds, levering their stout-black heads forward, before bombing into the sea, then ascending again. Down, then up. Down, then up, each like a feathered yo-yo. But this single gull loiters like lost love. I miss my uncle and the adventures we had together. Whitman's questions, the ones Therapist John shared with me, return to mind: *What do you stand for? What are you contributing to those around you? How will you be remembered?* Each question becomes like the repeated patter of feet on the surface of a road. But the personal fable, the heroic instinct, the grandiose ideas we men are hypnotised by, what do these matter if one day the sun will fry the human species anyway? I want to argue with Whitman, with Therapist John, with the past, the wind and anything or anyone who will listen: Why keep going? Why bother when loss hurts this much? What's the point? Two juvenile gulls heckle above my head as if arguing over a bad joke. Another with a misfit wing, like a book that hasn't been placed back properly on a shelf, lands at my feet and tries to gobble a pebble the size of a tennis ball. Does the dumb creature not realise?

There will be a full moon tonight, known to Native Americans as a Snow Moon, yanking the tide further up and further back than usual. Sea-wind stabs my cheeks so I clutch my body tighter, folding my arms into an X across my chest to stop my jacket from flapping. I imagine a map of the British Isles to join the geographic dots, east to west, from Brighton beach in the here-and-now where I squeeze myself like the Last Man Standing to Tenby beach where I clung to a cliff edge all those months ago. A coastline of nearly 300 miles separating two moments, traceable along a map as a single continuous line.

Two coasts, one map. Two moments, one mind.

Is this what we are doing in the background of our lives: Joining dots that have not been joined before? Reconciling fractures into a whole? Trying to make sense of things? Pecking at life like a pebble that won't yield?

Like many others, loss was my entry point into running long distances in the first place. We all have hearts which beat and loves which break. Watching a wooden box containing the cancerous bones of my mum sinking into a trench on a cloudy August day many years ago shook me. Running became a way through that first encounter with grief. I learned to run a long way by walking around the block, and little by little, metres became miles, and miles became marathons. My Uncle Andrew became my running mentor, advice-giver, looking up my results online and cheering me on from afar. In the next decade, inspired by his example and supported by my wife Hannah, I ran 20 marathons. First in London, then Dublin, Guernsey, Paris, and eventually three marathons in three consecutive days for a mental health charity of which I was the founder. On the third day I rose out of bed, legs and back aching so much I had to walk downstairs backwards. Arriving at the race start line on the High Street in Stratford-upon-Avon, I moved like a robot. Within the first mile I was over-taken by a man with a tumble dryer strapped to his back, a human turtle carrying the weight of the world. I trained as a Guide Runner for runners with visual impairments and as well as guiding others, in order to understand what it was like, I ran a few races blindfolded. I once ran a marathon dressed as a speed camera with a flashing head light attached to a vivid yellow cardboard box on my head, and a fifty-mile ultra marathon where I got lost in the Cotswold hills on the hottest day of the year. What I'm saying is - I was all in. Running long distances became an act of reorientation, a way of taming grief now I was motherless. If I kept striking my feet on the earth long enough I thought she might reappear, like tulips in spring.

Running teases us to go off the map, away from screens and demands of work and to relocate our equilibrium. "Ah, there I am" we seem to say at some indistinct point along the run. Running creates deliberate inconvenience and hassle, a thin, temporal protection from the comfort and collusions of modern life, levering us out of overthinking where the narrative can get tangled, selfish and small, returning us to the body-self and the wider frame of what is happening in the world. A marriage of physical and mental movement triggers insights, a portal into other places, perceptions, possibilities. Running wakes you up to your intrinsic resources, call it grit, where you have to locate your inside-strength to quieten the complaining-self and keep going. You face disturbance, you go in and through whatever struggle is on your mind, and emerge somehow renewed. Cognitive knots loosen. Sweat marks, blisters, aches, dirt all appear, yes, but you can never rewind to a time before the run. Your neural map changes a little with each run and the world stirs to life. Possibilities surface. You change to go running and then the running changes you.

"The point of life" said British philosopher Alan Watts, "is to be alive". I feel alive when I run, even when it is hard, especially when it is hard. When rain wrinkles the skin and wind screams in the ears. When all I hear is growls in my throat. Running is rarely comfortable, nor easy. When I run I feel rooted again in a swirling universe.

For a decade running became an act of self-coherence. Necessity, not luxury. Running was play and provocation (can you go further or faster?); it was purpose (the next race where glory awaits); it was partnership (hey, this is my tribe); and protection (from stress, boredom and illness). Running was a kind of free magic, a thread pulling me into the future, a thread as continuous as breathing amid whatever else occurred day to day.

But the thread stretched then snapped with the ending of married life, leaving the family home, no longer being a husband nor a dad living with his children, and whilst adjusting to these tectonic shifts, a difficult departure from long-term employment which tipped me into turmoil. In a sort of Copernican revelation, I was astonished to find that life revolved around something completely different to all I had believed for so long. The Small Self had clung on to an old story about who he was and how the world worked, but his time was up. I needed to get mentally sober from the well-rehearsed narratives inside my head. As psychologist Carl Jung said, "to get what we most need we have to look where we least want to look".

I'd hoped my first session of therapy would be a one-off pit-stop where I could offload my woes to a stranger I'd never see again before getting back up to speed and hauling in the medals. I considered myself A Strong Person. Hey, I ran Marathons. I knew about Endurance (I assumed Therapist John could hear the Capital Letters in what I said). To insist on always being the Helper and never the Helped proved a significant blind spot. "Be strong" the world shouts, but asking for help is the greatest show of strength, not because we need rescuing but because we are inextricably connected to one another. Helping is a polarity like breathing in and breathing out. We are designed for both: to help and to be helped.

"Slow down". Those were John's first words to me, having listened to my initial 50 minute monologue, my words racing against the clock. "Just...slow...down" he repeated, lowering both his hands towards the floor as if bringing traffic to a halt. There was a throbbing silence.

I wish there were pretty sentences to use, that the rage of losing what mattered to me, and the inevitable, necessary conflicts that followed, only lasted an afternoon. I wish that depression, post-traumatic stress disorder (PTSD) and episodic psychosis were still just terms in a dictionary. I have typed, deleted and re-typed that last sentence so many times. The fear of facing judgement is not theoretical. But I'm just another flawed human and the losses accumulated until my capacity to cope became overwhelmed. Eventually coping becomes exhausting and something has to give.

Losses ranged from the specific to the abstract and from the temporary to the permanent: loss of sleep; appetite; a lot of money; a car; a desk of my own and keys to the office; personal hygiene; daily routines; ability to concentrate; energy to run; time with my children and daily involvement in their lives; my contacts list; a wife's love and company; the loss of my uncle; the loss of feeling safe; confidence; a decent reputation and meaningful work; my home; being a husband; the loss of faith; loss of self-worth; loss of purpose. Yeah, I felt lost.

It was as if I'd exchanged all this loss for a question: "What's the point?" It didn't seem a great swap to be honest. But when life falls apart, however it happens, it is the same in the end. You have to sit with it, work it through somehow. The principle is to find something good from something hard.

Survive, Return, Restore.

In the story I've laid down upon these pages, what I found from hours of running across Tor-studded moors, beneath winter-sky meteors and through storm-wracked forests as a way to get through a long, hard time - the sort many people go through and I know many go through harder - often alone as I ran but not always, was that Walt Whitman's three questions presuppose something else left unsaid: that you are *Here*, fully pinch-yourself *Here*. Not lost in thought, nor entangled with the painful past. How else can you make the contribution that only you can make to those around you, unless you land fully in the here-and-now? Even now, all these years later abiding in the congruence of recovery, I have to remember: Life is only here and only now. The Ancient Greeks believed the future arrived from behind you, like a constant surprise, with the past existing in front of you, like scenery from which you are being extracted. Maybe it is only when we "Just... Slow...Down" that the underlying flow of life has a chance to catch up with us. Instead of living a life, life begins to live through us.

I began to wonder if Whitman's three questions might imply another question hiding between the syntax: "*Who are you becoming?*" A question leaning away from what's gone, who you were once upon a time, and instead moving you towards what's next, click-glide and trembling into your next moment, your unfolding future. "*Who are you becoming?*" is perhaps a more important question than who you were, back there. A question with an horizon you can reach for but never grasp. Maybe physical horizons are nature's way of giving us hope and if we pursue the horizon long enough we arrive where we belong. Or perhaps we miss the most obvious thing: that we stand upon an eternal horizon all along and there is nothing to chase.

By the evening Brighton Palace Pier is lit up and flashing like a disco. Walking through the twisting labyrinth known as The Lanes I find The Druid's Head, a pub coated in grey-cobbled stones, tucked away like a last resort. The bar maid, decorated up to her neck in tattoos, attends her phone, illuminating her face with temporary promises. The pub is empty except for a young lady who with her raspberry-dyed hair against a butter-coloured coat reminds me of a Mark Rothko painting, Red on Yellow. Her boyfriend walks in. She talks without pausing, fingers flicking, wrists gyrating, as if her gestures will conjure another drink. The boyfriend's attention, like the tide, is on its way out. A Miley Cyrus song plays over the sound system, something about "what goes up must come down". Miss Rothko stares at me. My head is all over the place so I wonder of which artist I remind her. Picasso perhaps? A number I heard on the news at breakfast time has my attention: 4,382, a number beyond one person's ability to de-code. It is as if something wants to step out from between the four digits and find voice. The number is how many men completed suicide in the UK last year, accounting for three quarters of all suicides (5,821). Those of us in the 45-49 age bracket are, statistically, the most at risk, the ones who most feel the absence of any brackets to contain them. According to Samaritans, a charity which exists to help those feeling suicidal, this figure is the lowest in three decades. Encouraging men to open up and seek help has contributed to the decline, but in another year the number will rise again, not only amongst middle-aged men but in younger females too. What goes down also goes up. Statistics rarely change us, but maybe stories can?

The varnished table wobbles when I lean upon it, spilling beer which runs off the table edge. My phone screen is bright with research about mental health and male suicide. I scroll down, down, down, a descent in search of original cause. There are trends. Demographic comparisons. Rates per 100,000 to adjust for population size. Risks associated with certain personality traits. Impact of emotional illiteracy. Economic factors, with unemployment and poverty as significant factors. The prevalence of stigma and resistance to help because many men feel tethered to the inherited and unexamined assumption to prove something, to be Superman. Some reports are decorated with academic language as if talking about lost units of production rather than brilliant, flawed human beings who were vulnerable. The danger is we become informed but not reformed. The scariest thing for many men is feeling power-less, which could be another word for depression. Perhaps this is why suicide deceives to be a rational option, a final act of self-power: "I can't succeed at anything else but I can at this." Yet my experience from over 10,000 hours of coaching conversations concerning mental health is that when someone experiences suicidal ideation, they don't usually want to be dead, just "dead for a bit". A rest from the onslaught, please. A chance to recover and get their breath back.

In truth, my introduction to suicide was a name not a statistic: the tragic death of a young man with whose family I lodged many years ago. Nathan had a photographic, mathematical memory and could recite pi to the 43rd decimal before the age of ten. He was barely out of his teenage years when he jumped from a plane for the first time. "When I jumped, everything happened fast" he wrote after his jump. "I took a moment to take in what was happening then my canopy opened and I was drifting gently to earth". We passed one another most nights in the kitchen when both hunting for supper, Nathan's long arms stretching up to the cupboard for a cereal box. Detecting my presence as an invasion of his privacy, Nathan would stare at the linoleum floor tiles during our staccato conversations before shuffling his feet upstairs with a cereal bowl balanced in one hand, and reunite with his best friend, a cat whose every move Nathan knew by heart.

A little more than two years after jumping from a plane Nathan used the twisted cord of his dressing gown to jump to earth from the loft hatch. His body dangled outside my bedroom door for a few hours whilst the rest of us were out of the house. I stared at the body that evening, resting without breath on a dark blue duvet creased like a tempestuous sea. No, not *the* body but *his* body, this precious body that once drifted gently to earth held safe by an open canopy. Pencil-grey indentations like bicycle tyre marks circled his neck from the cord. His skin as white as dried correction fluid. I stared at this young body who had the courage to parachute-jump and once flew a plane, who campaigned passionately for animal welfare, yet was too scared of people to use the university library. Nathan was autistic. He had gifts, perspectives and struggles those of us near to him didn't. Nathan felt he didn't fit in. Fitting in is something furniture is supposed to do, not people.

The house that evening murmured with Police speaking in short bursts of coded conversation. Radios crackled. Mugs of tea steamed on the dining table, then went stone cold. Was there more anyone could have done? I had mentioned to Nathan's father earlier that month, over chicken casserole covered in thin gravy, how it felt like there was a dark cloud over the house. I used those exact words, "dark cloud". I felt worry in my gut. I wasn't just his lodger, I worked half my week as this man's assistant gardener at a care home for the elderly. The father could not have loved Nathan more and I sometimes wonder if my presence in the house interfered with their bond. After the casserole dinner conversation, the father asked Nathan about how he was feeling. Things lightened in the home. But a few weeks later, it was the dressing gown cord and a life soaring from earth, as if ripped away.

In the months that followed Nathan's death it became difficult for the father and I to look each other in the eye as we passed the gravy jug across the dining table. Neither of us understood how grief had found its way in as the new lodger. As I closed my bedroom door at night there was a void in the white wooden frame, a gap where life should have walked past carrying a bowl of cereal. Several months later I moved out the house and we didn't speak to each other again, not on honest terms. Our friendship cooled in the winter-climate of grief, oxytocin levels plummeting, conversation stalling. We stopped asking "How are you?". I heard Nathan's father died recently. So much will forever remain unsaid.

Having suicidal thoughts, "suicidal ideation" as it is known, is increasingly common. According to the UK Government, on average around one in six people over the age of 16 have suicidal thoughts at some point. In a report by Samaritans, "Men and Suicide: Why it's a social issue", the way men are brought up to behave and the roles, attributes and behaviours that society expects of us is a significant contributing factor to men ending their life. Relationship breakdown, particularly, is more likely to lead men to end their life than women. We often don't have the same networks of support. Failing as a partner and/or father is like someone unplugging you from your power. Harmful assumptions can hide in the background causing you to feel like you don't have a place or role anymore - as if you don't fit. Job loss is another significant factor, the shame of failing to provide for your family, the betraying thought of "What are you worth if you can't even work and earn money?" Traditionally, men have more resistance to therapy or asking for help which may be beyond financial means when it would be of most benefit. Many men, but not all, carry an old burden of thinking we need to always Be The Strong One, avoiding vulnerability at all costs. In coaching work naming the emotions of this experience includes words and phrases like: *feeling empty; pulled down; powerless; cut off from others; stuck; totally lost; worthless; angry but too tired to show it; despairing; confused; sapped; numb.* These unpleasant yet intelligent emotions tell us "you have reached a limit and need rest." Don't try and power through. Accepting and showing vulnerability is a surprising route into genuine recovery and the revitalisation of true strength.

There is always the advice: *Talking helps. You are not alone.* This advice is profoundly true. Neuro-imaging using a SPECT scan has found less blood flows to the brain when someone experiences distress, when self-critical thoughts are in full throttle, particularly the cerebellum, cingulate gyrus and left basal ganglia (where the brain stores the coding for our habits and routines). We literally cannot think straight when we feel distressed. Empathic attention isn't a magic wand but it helps brains breathe, bodies relax and nervous systems settle.

According to recent annual surveys by Business In The Community of nearly 20,000 adults, the stigma around talking about personal mental health is still a major barrier to getting help. "Will people think there's something wrong with me?" we wonder, rather than "is something significant happening to me?". It is as if our internal antennae are bent toward caution and pathology rather than curiosity and potential. If we don't dismantle this stigma as adults, what example are we offering those who come after us?

Yet our capacity to help and heal one another is tremendous. Just seven minutes of emotionally attuned listening has shown to repair and rewire damaged neurons in the brain. In an accepting, empathic environment, where someone is perceived as an equal human, where their identity is respected and their experience validated, there is an increase in blood flow. This delivers more oxygenated blood, nutrients, and glucose to the brain which in turn calms the overactive amygdala (responsible for the well-known fight-flight-freeze response). The 40,000 neurons in the heart stimulate clearer decision-making in the pre-frontal cortex, often described as the CEO of the brain. Judgement and blame literally suffocate our thinking, whereas empathy and understanding resuscitate us.

Talking about how we truly are with someone we trust can keep us alive. In a way I got lucky. A neighbour, Murray, made time each week during a few intense months to walk with me to The Broom Tavern a mile up the road where we could not only talk about old cars and ex-girlfriends but attempt to make sense of the thing called "my former life" and the negativity which I couldn't quite shake off, like dog poo on the bottom of a shoe. But even solid friendships can't short circuit the fundamental process of personal change that still needs to happen. Moving through and beyond crisis into the next phase of life isn't as simple as turning over the record, from Side A to Side B. It takes time to see, understand and own the patterns which got us to where we are.

Froth sticks to the inside of the pint glass looking like an archipelago of exotic islands. I walk to the bar to buy another drink. Miss Rothko swings her coat around her shoulders and her boyfriend follows as if on an invisible leash, his nose three inches from his phone screen. As the pub door slams behind them, I return to my seat and tumble further into cyberspace. I come across the work of Claudine Herzlich, a Swiss psychologist who researched health and illness from the Middle Ages to the twentieth century. Herzlich's eyes, deep and dark like ink wells and framed in enormous spectacles, say "I see you". Herzlich does see things differently, asserting way back in 1973 that health is not merely an "absence of illness", but is "a presence of which one is fully aware". True mental health is a presence, a well of wellness, a source of serenity every single one of us can tap into which exists beneath the noise and narratives our discursive minds get tangled up in.

We say "it's good to talk", and it is, but when we can't find the right words, or words which feel safe enough, or true enough, we might assume those abstract things like meaning, purpose and identity have disappeared off the radar. The question *"Who are you becoming?"* could feel more like an accusation rather than an invitation. In your head the person you thought you were, with all the rules, roles, routines and relationships that knotted that old "self" together - "husband", "daddy", "the strong one" - all these labels stumble over the edge. Mentally, you feel spewed upon a distant shore, away from normality, whilst everyone else continues talking about normal things, like decorating the hallway and latest releases on Netflix.

I drain my glass. The buffering icon on my phone circles as web pages stay out of reach before connecting again, out of the blue. The World Health Organisation predicts depression will be the number one illness on the planet by 2030 and more prevalent than all the cancers combined. In the 21st century we are more inter-connected technologically than ever, yet we seem more disconnected from ourselves, from one another, and from the natural world we inhabit. As if soil, root, field, forest, heath, stream, rock, moor, meadow, mist, breeze are merely background scenery for our relentless activity, rather than the very substance within which we breathe, move and become. No wonder we are in a "mental health crisis" when our consumption-heavy lives are so divorced from the natural world. We seem to be caught in a collective state of buffering, round-and-round we go, getting stuck on the same old hurts, practising the same old useless reactions, using the same tired excuses for not changing our behaviour. We obsess about what we have, but are blind to the narratives we are had by.

Not all of this was going on in my head whilst scrolling my phone in The Druid's Head down a back lane in Brighton city centre, but most of it was. Angry, concerned, curious. The barmaid wipes beer-froth from the counter with a towel, her hand circling like a gesture of goodbye. I leave the pub, the wooden door shutting behind me with a grind of metal. On the way back to the hostel where I'm staying I notice the men sleeping against shop doorways (they all seem to be men), each curled foetus-like as if to rewind to a time when they were safe in their mother's womb. Some have pop-up tents on the pavement. One man has a ripped piece of cardboard leaning against the sole of his boots, a life story written in three sentences in thick black pen. The last line says "Thanx everyone for help at xmas" followed by a scribbled smiley face.

From Marine Drive I watch the black sea stumbling over itself. Flashing lightbulbs from Brighton Palace Pier reflect in the water, shattered fragments of light surfing upon the swell. I ran along this promenade on three occasions pushing my Uncle Andrew in his wheelchair, with no brakes, wheel suspension or fear. Twice we raced together in the half-marathon here, leading from the front for 30 seconds (the organisers thought it safer if we got out of everyone's way at the start), and once in the full marathon. The first time we raced he was dressed like he was about to climb Mount Everest, one hand clutching a chequered blanket over his knees, the other sounding an airhorn to warn other runners we were "Coming through!" He could still lift his right arm then.

Two runners, one motion.

Our marathon in Brighton together was his 40th marathon. That story will always feel like one of the greatest privileges I will ever have on earth. But it is finished. Away from the glaring lightbulbs, I enter the shoreline shadows. Shingle shifts beneath my trainers. The tide slams the shore, leaving a plastic bottle at my feet, a dented container divorced from its original contents with no secret message inside. Nothing feels certain anymore. Endings can bring confusion and reek of failure. Author Michael Neill says we can only fail in three ways: either we don't start to live in alignment with our true values; we give up too soon because it is hard (and revert to fitting in with everyone else) or we run out of time. "Follow your inner GPS" he says, listen to that quiet voice inside you, "and keep going". Keep searching for hints of what wants to happen next. Hold the question "what's emerging?" in your mind. My inner GPS says I need to run again.

The sssssshhhhh of the retreating tide over pebbles sounds like percolating coffee. I haven't run more than a few metres in the last year. My running trainers are hibernating at the back of a cupboard somewhere. "Without resilience, trauma triumphs" says Dr. Edith Grotberg, a pioneer in mental health research. Is that why we have to go all the way down sometimes, to find resilience, our "ordinary magic" as Ann

Masten phrased it, and claim it as our own? To find a space where the trauma can be seen and heard for what it was, allowing another larger story to emerge from the broken pieces? A newer truth reconciling the fractures into something whole, like a mosaic?

Along the beach through ink-darkness I run. Sea thrashes the stones. I run in old shoes designed for some other purpose, pumping my arms, my breath becoming short, feet careering on the unsteady surface. Nobody is watching this shadow stumbling along the shoreline. But the shadow moves and movement is proof of life.

After midnight I return to the hostel. Climbing the wide stairwell my saturated shoes tread on moonlight which floods the carpet, illuminating it like an Emergency Exit. Another traveller fills the dormitory with snoring as I clamber into the bunk beneath. Between his snores the tide outside sounds louder, as if something has turned.

This story is not about "fixing your mental health" because you don't need fixing. Neither is this a story of "Faster, Better, Stronger". Those stories are better told by others. If you detect any heroics in my words, then I have misled you. This is not a training textbook with latest advice on running plans, lactate thresholds or pronation shoes. All that is available elsewhere and useful to know if you intend to run any reasonable distance.

Recovering from loss, for me at least, meant uprooting from the identity and assumptions of the past and becoming anchored in the present. Running trails became a sanctuary, leading me around Loch Rannoch south of the Cairngorms in Scotland, up Snowdon's peak in Wales, through the Mourne Way mountains of Northern Ireland, and to all the cardinal points of the compass across England: Cheddar Gorge in the west, the fens in the east, the southern Jurassic coast, and around Kielder Water in Northumberland. I ran to hear, see and touch the unfamiliar, to join dots between childhood and adulthood and, by doing so, to make sense of those "confusing in-between phases of life" as William Bridges, originator of Transitions theory, called them.

We are easily distanced from contact with the land when moving across it at speed, hurtling from A to B, as if all the in-between places of life lack meaning. Land becomes felt only remotely, physical sensation diluted through rubber tyres and metal tracks. We move across something we barely notice as if the mind and body live a divorced existence. This story, for all its flaws, is an invitation to feel again what is both beneath, around, above and within you. It's just a story, a single data point, and we need many data points to get a truer picture of what it is to be human in these times. My intention here is not to convince you it's "like this" or "like that", but to provoke you into your own deeper truths. Please give it a shake. Test it against your experience. You know you better than I do. Notice what emerges for you as you read each page. How's it feeling so far?

Resurrecting my running kit from the cupboard was a good place to start but would be a poor place to finish. The landscapes I found myself running within triggered unplanned and surprising themes: liminality and loss; silence and wonder; attachment and nostalgia; depression and bliss; solitude and gratitude; memory and reflection. Like life, the themes are not linear. We don't exist in a tidy spreadsheet. This is a story about recovery, about how it can feel and what can help. As I found, recovery is not a solo quest, although it sure feels a lonely path. What the running became most of all was a lesson in learning to listen.

What follows is a conversation on the run across different landscapes. *Running Off The Map* unfolded at my feet and much of it was written (and re-written) on the move: on the return train from Pitlochry when the words first spilled out as sheer chaos; emailing myself from my phone as I ran through the icy December night, then up and down the Hayling Billy Line; recording voice messages running alongside Ladybower reservoir and whilst staring up at Snowdon; and typing whilst on a boat crossing Loch Lomond. And some of it was written in conditions of extreme quietness and solitude: curled up on a sofa during the first pandemic lockdown, often writing until dawn; lying alone in a tent on Tenby beach with just the shoreline and marooned jellyfish for company. In truth, the writing has been as much part of the recovery process as the running. As versions were revised, so the emotional tone turned from wounded to something more reconciled with reality, like feet gently landing upon the earth knowing the ground is safe again. Then after three years of (re)writing, the computer hard drive crashed when attempting to install a software update. I lost much of what I had written and gave up, tipping two box files of research notes into the recycling bin with an audible grunt.

The story went blank for over a year. A forced pause in the narrative. The metaphor didn't go unnoticed. Then my youngest son asked out of the blue one day, "Daddy, when are you going to finish writing that book?" Restoration is often a gradual gift: I retrieved information from photographs taken on the run, emails sent, journal notes, a decent paper version of the manuscript in the wrong box file. It was enough. My son's provocation to begin again means you now hold this in your hands.

With help I survived the loss of much which mattered to me. As we understand more, we forgive more: we forgive others, yes, but we also forgive ourselves for being human. To find a way of "returning" meant getting on a train at Birmingham New Street train station in rain that felt like pins piercing my skin, to go and run in one of the wildest places left in the British Isles.

Part II

IN SEARCH OF SANITY

AUTUMN

"The end is where we start from"

—T.S. Eliot

The train slows, squeals, stops dead. In the reflection of the train door windows I see myself split in two. I press "Enter" and a sound like forced exhalation causes the doors and my mirror image to part, left and right. I step into the gap, a human morsel entering the mouth of the train.

Doors snap shut behind me. Raindrops accelerate horizontally across the window as the train rests in New Street Station. They begin as dots, but as the train jerks, hums and gathers speed the dots accumulate, becoming like transparent sperm, tails wagging with excitement, racing to the edge of the frame as if seeking escape. Between tower blocks clustered like tenpins the English Midlands landscape chokes in cloud. Everything has the appearance of being contained: this string of boxed metal carriages coupled and clasped, clanking past concrete-tiered car parks; brown-brick houses chained together in rows; a cemetery heaving with gravestones, lop-sided like bad teeth. The train coughs through Wolverhampton, Crewe, eventually wheezing into Preston. The train is old and moves with a feeling of regret.

The stomach of the man next to me ripples generously over the edge of the table so I too am boxed in. The word PSYCHOCANDY is printed across his t-shirt, twice, one above the other, with the N of CANDY in mirror image so *together the letters look like an arrow pointing at a wall. I notice in the window's reflection the book resting beneath my palm, fingers splayed across its cover, my wrist vertical and trunk-like, as if my body and the wood of words on the pages are all one story, flowing upward, branching out in thought.*

It is an eight hour journey to Kinloch Rannoch, just south of Scotland's Cairngorms, home to pine martens, red deer and golden eagles. Loch Rannoch, around which the marathon event route is set, is surrounded by an expanse of peat-bogged moor larger than the entire English Lake District. Judging by the photospheric map on my mobile phone runners will become tiny blue dots, racing east to west through the Black Wood of Rannoch towards the desolation of Rannoch Moor. The saxophone of John Coltrane's "Blue Train" fills my headphones. Rain withdraws to the sky.

"Look at that!" I yelp, my fingers flinging arrow-like to beyond the window frame toward a sunken waterfall where the hillside has burst a seam, as if something living wants to break through. My gasp causes PSYCHOCANDY Man to look up from his book, a sturdy book about how the human brain is a computer, its pages suffocated with diagrams, grids, boxes, as if trains of thought can be caged in typeface. His spectacles slide down his nose. He snorts, before fixing his glasses back in place with his index finger, pointing at himself between the eyes like an accusation. The stream weaves alongside the train tracks, water music muted by the metal cacophony of the machine in which we sit. It keeps pace, as if in chase, with something urgent to say to us, but the train stays fixed on ==== wherevernext==== wherevernext==== wherevernext==== as if our destiny is in question.

PSYCHOCANDY Man falls asleep, snores erupting then escaping through curled lips. An electronic voice projects itself over our heads, announcing we will soon be in Carlisle. He re-awakes as if from cardiac arrest and grasps his book (which was snoozing face down, pages doing the splits and creasing the spine). He levers himself up from the seat, before stumbling from the train. As the train grunts back to life, I watch him turn 360 degrees on the platform, a suitcase in each hand like scales of justice, an automatic rotation that pleads: "Where the hell am I?"

I think about PSYCHOCANDY Man's book and begin to wonder about this idea that the human mind is like a computer. But computers don't have feelings, understand intuition, accommodate fascination, nor embrace sorrow. They can't open themselves to mystery, ignite inspiration, offer mercy, or face regret. It is all pre-programmed response. Computers do not breathe, cannot forgive. They don't gasp at a waterfall or express spontaneous appreciation. I think about PSYCHOCANDY Man handcuffed to his suitcases, spinning on the platform at Carlisle, as if the human programme can't tolerate uncertainty and prefers instead to go round in circles of perpetual motion just to keep busy. Just to avoid feeling the truth of being human.

Sheep graze unaware of this metal tube of humans penetrating their ancient pastures. Rocks mark where walls once were. Hills rise, fall, rise again. Staring out the window, I recall the story of Roger Ulrich who as a teenager suffered kidney disease. Ulrich noticed how seeing a pine tree from his hospital bedroom window helped lift his mood, acting like medicine for the mind. Later in his life Ulrich became curious whether other people experiencing fear and stress in hospital would benefit from views of trees and water. His pioneering research in 1984, precisely titled "View through a window may improve recovery from surgery", found those with access to natural views, namely deciduous trees and water, needed less pain relief and fewer dosages after surgery. They also left hospital sooner. Ulrich's research, specifically about 23 patients in a Pennsylvanian hospital, suggested that natural views "sustained interest", "reduced stress" and "fostered restoration from anxiety". I believe him. Last week in a school, a teenage girl with hair that hung like weeping willow said to me it was staring out the geography classroom window at trees in the school playground which helped her mourn the loss of her grandad. "They just stand there, don't they, and sort of help" she said, "it's a bit like mental Wi-fi with nature" and she laughed, the spirals of her hair bouncing as if revived. There is an old Czech proverb: "As long as the language lives, the nation survives." We talk about people having "breakdowns"; "recharging our batteries"; people "pressing our buttons".

We say "the cogs aren't turning"; someone has "a screw loose"; we want to "switch off". We talk as if people are photocopiers in need of repair. If the language lives, the idea survives. All humans hope, grieve, yearn, lose, worry. None of us are robots. Maybe it takes loss to crash the old mental programmes, to ditch our inherited scripts and our futile addiction to chasing achievement and instead go searching for a new way of being in the world. To travel as a pilgrim rather than a tourist, learning how to notice rather than accumulate. Humans are not machinery with buttons and levers, regardless of how mechanically cluttered our vocabulary becomes. All the vast, astonishing sights out there - the stars, valleys, forests and seas - all this stirs something deep within our own nature, because we are nature.

The train darts northward towards Edinburgh, enduring a long stretch without a station, an in-between zone where anything feels possible. The coffee cup sits empty, wanting a refill. As I ready to leave the train at Edinburgh to collect a hire car to Pitlochry I wonder what new connections might be waiting, what new streams of thought might flow, like Coltrane's jazz, and whether PSYCHOCANDY Man ever found a way off the platform . Perhaps he is still spinning.

Opening the bedroom door of the Pitlochry hostel I am confronted by a concerning sight.

LOCH RANNOCH

Life is not straight forward

"It's room number two, up the stairs, turn right", Ian, the hostel receptionist says upon my arrival. "Ya sure you don't want these wee things?" he asks, waving ear plugs as I mount the stairs. I push the door open. The malodour of feet is only surpassed by the sight of a man, almost seven feet tall, in saggy blue Y-front pants. "Hello. I'm Max, but don't get me confused with the other Max". He checks whether I speak English, then without pausing for breath tells me how windy it was in a bothy on the Isle of Skye and what the hostel kitchen downstairs is like. Max is as pale as frozen chicken, his blue eyes and strawberry-red nipples protruding like unrelated landmarks. "Make sure you label your milk otherwise some wanker will steal it" he warns. Note to self: don't use Max's milk. I don't sleep well, longing for Ian's ear plugs, as two men called Max compete for prize of Top Snorer.

The day before the marathon I walk up East Moulin Road, past Moulin Brewery where they brew Braveheart ale, until at the town boundary, at the crest of a hill, I turn and see hills scarfed in mist. The peak of Ben Vrackie is nowhere in sight but through the mist-veil are stanzas of blood-red maples, birches the yellow of English mustard and beeches the colour of caramel. Returning to the hostel, saturated from walking through a fuzz of rain, Max (version 2.0) has kindly raised the window halfway so male foot odour leaks into the Pitlochry rain and by exchange the Pitlochry rain soaks my bedding.

Race day. 5.00 a.m. My bare feet rest upon a rung of the bunk bed ladder as I try not to wake my dormitory companions. Y-Front Max is spread-eagled on top of his duvet looking and smelling like roadkill. Snoring suggests he is alive. I creep downstairs, sip black tea, eat porridge and from a pinewood bench watch the the clandestine emergence of day as the shadowed ridge of Pitlochry's hills beyond the River Tummel become distinct from the night, land and sky teasing themselves apart like peeling a sticker from its backing.

The road to Loch Rannoch passes through Killiecrankie, hugging the edge of Cairngorms National Park. Distracted by immense fists of rock protruding into the road with water lolloping down their seams I miss the turn, twice, before arriving at Muirlodge Place next to Loch Rannoch. An Old Church of Scotland building rests beside a large beech tree. Eight cars are parked on the well-kept football pitch. The lady at the check-in desk, which is just a wobbly trestle table beneath a temporary gazebo, tells me 160 runners have entered the race, of which 108 eventually turn up. There is a buzz in running crowds of 30,000 in big city marathons, a voltage of enthusiasm that sky-rockets your dopamine levels, but today has a different vibe. It is intimate rather than anonymous.

Schiehallion, one of Scotland's best known hills at 3553 feet high, erupts from the landscape like a circumflex, a small neckerchief-like cloud loitering beneath its peak. In 1774, with the backing of the world's oldest scientific institution, The Royal Society, British astronomer Revd. Nevil Maskelyne performed an experiment on Schiehallion using a plumb line to accurately determine the density of the earth. You wouldn't want to compete with Maskelyne for guess the weight of the cake at the village fête. Maskelyne's experiment gave rise to the invention of contour lines on maps by Charles Hutton, a miracle of making the invisible visible.

"Excuse me, do you know where the start line is?" a man asks. We look for a sign together, both of us turning in full circles like a game of pin the tail on the donkey. He spots a huddle of coloured running vests a hundred metres away. There are no runners in fancy dress, just dozens of shivering bodies, some wrapped in dustbin liners or silver foil blankets to keep warm. As we approach the group a hire van skids to a halt next to us. A man in soaking wet trousers leaps out and with a metal mallet strikes metal posts into the ground either side of the dirt track. Then he slams down a pile of thick red mats, each action creating an echo in the hills. A lady one third his size joins him, poking flag banners into the soft ground. With minutes to go the race start line is constructed before our eyes. Out of nothing a way takes shape. The visible world of posts, mats, flags, signs, cones, illuminates the invisible, bringing the contours of the marathon map to life.

Wet Jeans Man calls us together. "Come closer, you can warm each other up with your body heat" he says, and there is a rustling sound as runners huddle. "We have had to change the course due to last nights flooding. The south side of the loch is not passable" and he points to tide marks on his jeans as evidence of how deep the water is in places. "I've not had, you know, a little accident" he reassures us. "You will run along the north side of the loch, go round a traffic cone, then run back again." Runners groan. He explains how we will need to run across the start line (which is still being built), run a loop, then come back across the start line, "then" he says "you'll do another loop to a different traffic cone and come back across the start line. Again". This is the most confusing beginning to a race I've ever heard. The start line is now a real thing with mats to record chip timing and flags flicking in the breeze sounding like slow applause. Wet Jeans Man yells a countdown from ten then honks a hooter and we begin. A broken line of spectators watch as we cross the start line, once, twice, three times, moving haphazardly towards the 10 mile-long tongue of Loch Rannoch.

Passing Annat Burn and the gathering of Laganiasgair Cottages after four miles, a man called Lucas with the gentlest of voices runs alongside me. "I was born in the Shetland Isles" he tells me, "those islands people put in a box on the map because they're so far north". We overtake a runner in his sixties with a Charles Darwin-like beard and his eyes tight shut. His running top announces he is from the Orkney Islands. "How far away are they?" I ask Lucas. "From Stromness, that's 200 or so miles north of here, but this might be his local race." Whenever I see the Orkney Racer during the run his eyes are closed as if channelling magical powers from Schiehallion. Lucas started running to lose weight. "I hated running if I'm honest with you because it was hard work, but mates encouraged me. That's all it took, once or twice a week, someone saying 'you can do this'". We run together at ten minutes per mile pace, which feels okay for now. The winner will eventually finish in 2 hours 42 minutes, evidence of how little undulation there is along the loch's north side. "This is my sixth marathon" Lucas says, lifting his chin and laughing as if to say "if only I knew then what I know now!" Occasionally Lucas stops because he has "that feeling...you know..." before disappearing behind a tree, crunching through toffee-coloured bracken in order to see to nature's call. I stop and stare at the loch's silver skin, one hundred metres deep at its deepest point. Feet beat past in a steady rhythm behind me, runners in clusters, their heads down as if the road can't be too trusted. An old rowing boat with the number 34 painted on its side sits near to the loch edge, solitary and mute. Its twin image is captured in exact form and cast upon the water in reverse. It is the only object I see upon the loch all day. The unpunctured surface hides everything beneath and reflects everything above, a mirror in the landscape holding the sky in its wet palm.

There can be something inherently restorative about being near, in, or on water, a sort of spirit level for the mind. The presence and sight of water can influence our thinking and improve our well-being. Roger Deakin, co-founder of environmental charity Friends of the Earth, suggested expanses of water, like the loch, act as a metaphor for freedom, offering us space to think. "It is the only opportunity we have in the landscape to see a truly level flatness" he said, for "the rest of the landscape is always spiky, full of virtual lines... grass, trees, hills, buildings, people." Water spaces offer a breather from the intrusions of buildings and machinery, a visibly flatter line in the environment to settle our minds, helping brain waves to shift down gears and settle into a flow.

This is a landscape without intrusion, where sky-space and mountain stillness invite the mind into a gap. A stream of serenity emerges from somewhere beneath the analytical mind. Something shifts as "life out there" (what I can see and hear) and "life in here" (what I feel and sense) tune into one another. The invisible contours of Being are redrawn.

As Lucas reappears from peeing behind a tree a veil of cloud dissipates and a white warm sun flashes on us, like a camera. For a time I feel that rare thing of being dissolved in the landscape and the landscape becoming more vibrant within me. We probably all experience these moments, often fleeting and serendipitous, but a testament to there being something beyond the noise of our brains. The solidity of the earth beneath each step becomes a direct, bright and immediate confirmation of being Alive. It's so easy to miss this, forever getting caught up in problems and pressures, many of which haven't even happened.

As we run, east to west, I ask Lucas about living on Shetland. "It's just lots of space. All my family live there, farming, but I'm the black sheep for having left the island in the box. I didn't want to continue with what had always been done before. I had to break out, y'know." For several miles we just run in a synchronous rhythm alongside one another, absorbing the stillness of the landscape, moving through nature, and nature moving through us. Beyond 11 miles we run beneath birch trees whose leaves hang like handfuls of gold coins, a hive of honey yellows coating the road. I have an urge to touch everything to check it is real.

Crossing the Bridge of Ericht we pass a mill towards where the loch thins into the River Gaur. We are confronted by a clan of forty mallards squabbling as they rush toward the feet of a man whose gangly height and stick-thin frame makes him look like he is made out of pipe cleaners. He reminds me of Roald Dahl's BFG. Standing upon his farmhouse doorstep he scatters grain to the ducks chorusing at his feet. He sees us and waves with vigour, perhaps the only humans he will see all day. His arm sways in giant arcs, specks of grain launching into the air like fireworks, causing the ducks to go berserk.

Because of the previous nights flooding and the route change explained by Wet Jeans Man, to reach the official marathon distance of 26.2 miles we are guided by a marshal over the Bridge of Gaur, then down and back up several puddled tracks marked with traffic cones. The Orkney Racer passes us coming the other way, his eyes still closed, still searching… searching… for himself perhaps? We turn at a cone marking the halfway race point and pivot toward the finish line. The route to the finish mirrors the route from the start as precisely as the loch mirrors the features of the landscape. The first half is complete, the second half opens up.

It was only on the train back from Edinburgh whilst browsing on my phone that I discovered that the word "loch", meaning "nearness of shore", comes from the Greek word *limne* and the Latin *limbus*, giving us the words "limbo", "limitation", "liminality" and "limbic" (often used to describe the middle part of the human brain). We say we are "in limbo" when we feel aimless, not sure what to do or where to go. Liminality also derives from the Latin word *limen* (I know, there's lots of Latin here, but origins reveal meaning). *Limen* means to "occupy a position at, or on, both sides of a boundary or threshold". In the middle ages, the threshold was the piece of wood at the bottom of the door frame which "held the thresh", the golden straw from the field, like medieval carpet rods. Liminality feels like being suspended between old and new. The coronavirus pandemic introduced many of us to levels of liminality we had never previously known where the rules of normal life were put on hold. Life went off the map as assumptions about how life worked were obliterated. Do you remember? Old certainties ended, liminality arrived and most of us freaked out. Experiencing liminality for anything more than a short period of time is hard for human brains that are wired for survival and certainty, wooed by a belief that we always have to know what we're doing and where we're going. "Destination addiction" as author Rob Holden calls it. But liminality also means "to be sitting on the gold". In the most pronounced liminal stages of life we cling to the edges of what we know, not appreciating this can be a significant turning point. Uncertainty can become a fertile place enabling possibility. If we want to understand mental health better and help anyone (including ourselves) we must understand the nature of liminality and learn how to live with it, live through it and learn deeply from it, because liminality is woven into reality and is the doorway through which the future comes.

Okay, a confession: Writing about liminality has been the hardest part of this whole thing. My dad said, after reading an early draft, "I got lost in that bit about liminality, Chris", as if even reading about it conjures up the experience of the very thing that's trying to be pinned down. Liminality, with its bewildering dynamic ('be-wilder'), is uncomfortable for brains raised on binary positions: good/evil; right/wrong; success/failure. Many of us resist "not knowing" and the blurred in-between with all our might, evident in our insistence to know things in advance and defend our view when challenged by difference. Yet experiencing liminality is necessary for any significant transition to accomplish its intrinsic purpose. In gestalt psychology it's known as "the fertile void".

Liminality gets confused with boredom, passivity, and resignation, which may all feature, but it is none of these things in itself. Liminality is more familiar to us than we might credit ourselves. We experience shallow types of liminality everyday in the easy-to-miss transitions between doing one thing and another, waiting in a shopping queue or at a traffic stop light. It is in the slumber of nighttime between one day and the next. We feel it in the short gap between one breath ending and the next beginning. The volatility of the teenage years ("in-between-ages") is a prolonged liminal stage of life to which many of adults wouldn't ever want to return. But deeper liminality often occurs during a significant personal transition when we are between jobs, homes, geographies, relationships, genders, the menopause or a life-stage change. Those times when certainty and "normality" jump out the window. "The change is external, but transition is internal" says William Bridges. Whether we like it or not, life is not straight forward, leaping from one certainty to the next. It has to be messy for it to continue. Bereavement is a reliable harbinger for liminality as loss-related emotions pull us this way and that, much of it outside our conscious awareness so we end up thinking (unhelpfully) something is wrong with us.

Here's the thing: We need to be reassured of how common liminality is, especially in the mid-life stages, and how necessary it becomes to find safe people with whom to share the reality of our experience. During transitional stages of life when a significant thing has ended but something new hasn't yet begun we might spend more time awake at night, as if tipped into the underworld where darker thoughts loom larger than normal: "oh my god, what if...?" (worry); "why on earth did I...?" (guilt); "right, I'm going to..." (revenge); or "what's the point?" (low mood). These thoughts become more intense, insistent and persuasive than ever. This mental merry-go-round can be exhausting and frightening. Perhaps you've experienced this but never told anyone? It is no surprise that the risk of psychosis, depression and suicidal ideation all increase with liminal experiences, which was the case during the pandemic. Personal recovery and healing do not come with a "Just Hit Turbo" option. They require time, wisdom and help from others. Visiting the doctor might be necessary. Accessing therapy is another option, a structured liminal place to help expand awareness and choice. A turning inward to find the way forward. ("If only each sentence would follow neatly on from the last" I keep thinking as I type and edit for the umpteenth time).

Liminal places appear abundantly in fairytales, myths and sacred texts to remind us of their necessity in the journey of human development. There's the island of Calypso in "The Odyssey" where Odysseus washed up on a shoreline, taking sanctuary on his return journey during which he was blown around the Mediterranean (meaning "middlelands") for three years; there's the belly of a whale that swallowed the prophet Jonah (a place within a place, hidden beneath the surface of the sea); the deserts that Moses, Jesus and Mohammad endured for their transformation; the seas in Moby Dick; the forest in Midsummer Night's Dream. In Greek myths, Persephone, goddess of spring, oscillated between underworld and overground, always on the edge of one or the other. It is no accident that many of these "confusing nowhere places", to use William Bridges' phrase, are often located within nature away from human crowds: an island, a whale belly, deserts, seas, forests, underland spaces. Liminality intensifies aloneness because something significant is going on.

Liminality is not just a concept in developmental psychology but is *revealed first* in nature. You have seen and felt this, for sure. The natural world all around us froths with transformative, liminal processes: the in-betweenness of dawn and dusk; hibernation; transitions between seasons (especially winter to spring); fermentation; photosynthesis. "Things go slowly for a time and nothing seems to happen" says William Bridges, "until suddenly the eggshell cracks, the branch blossoms, the tadpole's tail shrinks away, the leaf falls, the bird molts." When a caterpillar creates a chrysalis to undergo the process of changing into a butterfly, the caterpillar doesn't just pop fresh wings on like a change of evening attire. The caterpillar disintegrates into sludge, it becomes a No-Thing (becoming 'nothing' is a great human fear). The butterfly, which in some faiths symbolises resurrection, emerges from this total decomposition, gradually forming as an entirely new creature. What leaves the chrysalis is something altogether different from what went in. The butterfly's wing-strength is forged as it fights its way out of the self-made grave. Likewise, our struggle with the enforced limitations of liminal times is necessary for developing our own strength. Many people will do anything to avoid the disruption that liminality brings, investing effort in staying on cruise control and capsizing the prospect of anything new beginning by conjuring up a hundred worst case scenarios. Change triggers transition, and transition surfaces our deepest worries, fears and attachments. We must notice the transition that's going on beneath the thing we *think* is going on.

However hard we try we only change by going *through* the loss and uncertainty of change, we can't jump over ourselves to become someone different or click, swipe, download the new version of who we are becoming. A Better Version of You isn't going to show up by writing to Father Christmas. And when things don't change, or not in the way or timeframe we anticipate, the frustration inherent within liminality can get tangled up with feeling powerless: "I want something to change, I should be able to control this" (we secretly think) "but I can't control the change". When the ideal outcome we have imagined proves out of reach, the change-impulse might get turned outward into blame and acting out, or inward triggering an urge toward self-harm, shame and sometimes suicidal ideation and action. We need safety valves for this kind of pressure, especially when the timeframe of "Not Knowing" is prolonged. "Hope deferred makes the heart sick" as the old proverb goes.

And here's my point: Keeping the difficulties of liminal experiences hidden in one's own headspace won't help. The tongue has a role to play and private thoughts need oxygen, especially those weighted with shame, fury, and worry. Asking for help isn't just okay - it becomes vital. Liminality confronts us with our limitations and proves, eventually, that we can only move forward with the help of Another. The paradox is that feeling lost helps us find our way.

Liminality can feel troubling because it takes us to the edge of our mental maps, revealing the boundaries and assumptions we have lived by but then bump up against. None of us know for sure what tomorrow brings. Limitations - to our knowledge, power and control - are frustrating before they become liberating. German philosopher Karl Jaspers says we can tell we are facing a "limit situation" because we experience intense dread, guilt, doubt or anxiety, and a great burden of responsibility. The brain experiences a boundary where a neurological pathway doesn't yet exist - some have said they experience this as an ache toward the back of the head as if part of the brain is in a struggle of some kind. When the old controls no longer work, emotions go haywire and personal resources get sucked dry.

We can't make sense of everything in one go, but we do have to sit with the uncomfortable uncertainty awhile, allow it to do its work and learn to follow its lead. One of its gifts is to teach us to trust something deeper than the rational brain, something in the gut, something intuitive, our inner sense. Intelligence ascends from lower down (gut and heart) to higher up (brain), like summiting a mountain. In fact 400 times more information is ascending than the other way around. The topsy-turvy nature of liminality helps get us the right way up.

Emotions contain motions, moving from one to another. Genuine internal change means leaning into this uncomfortable uncertainty and encountering its nature: *lostness, confusion, frustration, turbulence, limitations, surprise, expansion, synchronicity, losing control* and *needing to trust*. In coaching conversations when someone is experiencing liminality which is paralysing their sense of choice (often like a tug of war about whether to do this or do that), it helps to draw up two lists: the first list is of all the things you can't control or influence but which may be dominating your attention. The second list is of what *is* within your control or influence, including of what you can let go. Choice includes what you don't say or do. People are surprised that the second list is longer than the first and reveals the easy-to-miss controls often hiding in plain sight: your breathing, attention and intention, your curiosity, posture and energy, a simple request or next step. We must return to the centre of our Being, again, again, again. The whole process is non-linear, non-rational, non-controllable. No wonder liminality does our heads in.

The first time I heard the word "liminality" was over coffee with a friend, the word buzzing in the air like a wasp magnetising my attention. Something in my gut felt apprehensive (and rightly so). A year later I arrived full throttle at the limits of my own self-made map of how I believed the world worked and nothing made sense anymore. A close friendship of 20 years broke down. I felt betrayed by them. The realisation of being lied to was like a blindfold ripped from my eyes. I screamed so hard as I drove home that I lost my voice for a week. Despite feeling terrified by the threats I faced, I did speak out, because ethically that was the appropriate thing to do, but loyalties are complex and it took over two years for the truth to come to the surface. Maybe it had to be that way. I experienced the shadow side of religion which ruptured my worldview. Suicidal ideation became intense for five months, like a thud at the front of my brain, as if something was trying to get the hell out of there. This was a ferocious shock because I never considered myself to be "the sort of person" who would have those kind of thoughts. I was helped when a friend mentioned, whilst out walking hills together, that they had experienced suicidal thoughts in the past. Naming it out loud was freeing and softened the deep sense of rejection I felt from those I had known and trusted. I recently saw the former friend drive past me. They looked weathered. "May you be well" I said quietly, hoping the energy of the words might penetrate their car windshield.

Somewhere in the mayhem of my adjustments, I chanced upon the kindness of friends who agreed I could sleep in their refurbished shed, formerly a small stable, rent free (I say "shed", but it had a tiled floor, a single wall-mounted heater, mattress with hand-knitted cushions on and I could squeeze my £6 clothing rail from Asda inside). The night I moved in, paused on their television screen as I walked through their lounge, was the title of a programme they were watching when I knocked on their door: "Safe House". At that moment I needed that sign.

Through the shed window, morning by morning, without work or the energy to get out of bed before dusk, I observed the slow metamorphosis of a cherry tree shedding its scarlet leaves so they lay like a pool of blood at its base. I watched its branches become bereft and burdened by snow, until its own transition led to pink blossom-fingertips emerging once more. I was about to turn 44 years old: a number full of straight lines, structure, points and interesting angles. Everything that was missing from my life. My "life" broke, like the straps on a satchel that has carried too much for too long. Why am I telling you this? Because recovery begins with stark raving honesty. As American nun Pema Chödrön says, it comes as "a great relief when we get to drop the act".

That winter, surviving in the shed at the crescendo of a divorce process which lasted exactly 1000 days, trying to sell the family house, disentangling from conflict and confusion at work, not earning a penny but dealing with three different solicitors, the betrayal of a close friend and feeling paranoid about the threats - that winter snow fell as if the heavens were disintegrating. I walked through field after field, through gates and over stiles like a solo hunter in search of hope, footprints crunching deep impressions in snow only to be obliterated within minutes. I wanted to shake a fist at everything and everyone, especially the man in the mirror. "When you gaze into the abyss" wrote German philosopher Frederick Nietzsche "the abyss gazes into you." Many nights I awoke in distress gasping for breath, chest heaving, a weight suffocating my body. A dark presence filled the room at night for a year, something I can only describe as evil, however unscientific that sounds. At night I grasped the bed frame with both hands, shaking it like a prisoner at a barred window, before collapsing onto the mattress, sobbing. "Before we can see properly" says an Indian proverb, "we must first shed our tears to clear the way". I wept in private every day for months until there was nothing left. I understand now that a "good" cry is not a sign of weakness. Crying restores the thinking process by activating the parasympathetic nervous system helping blocked emotions get flushed out and releasing oxytocin (the attachment, nurturing neurochemical). There also comes a time to stop crying, to put a boundary around it and say "okay, no more. Rest now." Too much crying leaks the energy you need for recovery. Pulling at one thread in the web of life sends tremors across the whole system. Who knew it could all unravel so easily? When my family asked "How are you?" I said I was "continuing", like digestion, photosynthesis or the rotation of the earth. My family and few remaining friends were a refuge, cooking meals and offering sofas to sleep on when the "shed" was needed for other matters. My family withheld judgement and I owe them gratitude for their help during that time. I learned that living in line with your true values comes at a cost, and I lost much that I loved. The "shed" became my home for five months until my family house sold and I was able to rent a tiny flat on the same road where I had lived.

On some level, understanding that my circumstances had stumbled into a Liminal Zone kept me alive, offering protection from the frightening, insistent thoughts that I should end it all, because "my life" (as it had been constructed) felt at an end. It was *An Ending*, not *The End*. On better days I had a way of answering those dark thoughts back: "I know you feel out of synch with everyone else, but this is liminality. Just do today what you can. Wash. Brush your teeth. Walk to the end of the road and back". An adult voice, not quite as coherent as that written sentence, but a wiser self perhaps, taking care of a wounded me who felt *empty, powerless, defeated...numb*. Just being aware that liminality with all its confusing in-betweenness is a natural, inevitable feature in the process of personal growth helps validate the experience. There IS a purpose. An old set of assumptions are dying so a new way of being can emerge. Liminality moves us toward what psychologist Carl Rogers described as "more complexity, more order, more inter-relatedness". You become more, not less: more whole, more healed, more vibrant, more grounded, more true. The endless loops of self-criticism soften. You drop down from survival mode into something far deeper, a flow of life which carries you. "Understand that this in-between condition" wrote poet Seamus Heaney at the turn of the millennium in his commencement address at the University of Pennsylvania, "is not to be regarded as a disabling condition... it is rather a necessary state, a con-

 of our situation between earthy origin and angelic potential."
ity feels like nowhere but it activates a recalibration to being

Now-Here. You yield to the process and slowly the vitality of life can return. You notice you really ARE here, even though here is nowhere in particular.

By the loch, Lucas and I run alongside one another in silence, footsteps and breathing in rhythm, determined to reach the finish line. We are two dots on a map, a unifying force moving horizontally over the path. Eighteen miles run becomes nineteen, slowly turning to twenty. Each mile feels longer than the last as if unraveling from the spindle of eternity. Lactate acid accumulates in both knees. The peak of Schiehallion is lit orange like a candle in the afternoon sun, keeping vigil for our return. We duck beneath the draping birch tree branches whose gold leaves fall like confetti upon us. The nearer we get to the finish, the more the trees sag with the anticipation of winter, sensing the inevitable loss of all it has clung to these past months. Nature readies itself for the nowhere zone, again, when many things (but not all), will fall, fade, hide, hibernate, disintegrate or die, awaiting Persephone's touch to stir them into renewed life in five months time. The landscape here reminds me that loss isn't failure, that letting go contains the first reconnections of spring.

We run past the sleeping church, beneath the priestly beech which guards its entrance and together cross the race finish line. Lucas and I lean upon one another in the empty football field, exhaling relief and smiling at having finished the marathon, by a matter of seconds, in under four and a half hours. A lady approaches a few moments later, tucking the dark curls of her fringe behind her ear. "Why do you *do* this sort of thing" she asks, admitting she feels perplexed by the whole event. Between tired breaths I say something about "starting life again". She laughs, pointing at my race number. Pinned to my t-shirt is the number 1234. "Your number says it all!" she says.

Back in Pitlochry, I walk a mile downhill, across the bridge over the River Tummel and up Port-Na Craig Road. I want to see the Salmon

Ladder, a chain of wood-planks which look like an escalator of HHH-HHHH attached to the river bank. Salmon take this route to find their way up river to re-spawn, obeying their instinct to go against the flow. Standing on the dam, gazing downstream, the river surface is a shoal of silver scales winking in the early evening sun. I'm not ready just yet to return to the hostel and face Y-front Max. I really shouldn't have used his milk for my porridge this morning. Failing to see any leaping salmon (it's the wrong time of year), I shuffle into town to find something to eat. Over a pizza piled high with haggis in the cosy Café Biba, I open the book I bought in the John Muir Trust bookshop yesterday: "When I wrote the following pages, or rather the bulk of them" begins the story, "I lived alone, in the woods, a mile from any neighbour, in a house which I had built myself…" I wonder if this is going to be a story about hobbits, magical rings and a large flaming eye scouring mythical lands. A story about how little folk find they are at the centre of some epic tale, but it is not. It is about Henry David Thoreau living in a shabby cabin over 170 years ago. A man who wandered off the map for a while.

When I leave the restaurant an hour later, I haven't got past the first page of the book. My brain is too tired and the pint of beer too good. I need to return to the hostel before my legs seize up. Clenching the book under my armpit, I ease the café door open and stumble onto a street without light. The night clouds have collapsed and a thousand bright eyes are watching.

WINTER

"Stuff your eyes with wonder"
—Ray Bradbury

Something happens on the return journey from Pitlochry. One trail marathon isn't going to be enough. I feel chronically out of shape but an idea is planted which over the coming weeks sprouts into a plan. I can't just keep sitting in a chair with a therapist and work it all out. Life is not Sudoku. I have to go and get lost somewhere, confront elements, expose my fears to the open air, not just rehearse them in hushed conversations in the corner of a room. I need space to scream and pound my feet into the earth. I have to grieve: for my marriage, for no longer living with my children, for my uncle, broken friendships, for the ending of 40 years of loyalty to religion. To grieve is to acknowledge you loved and lost. To grieve is to grow. Therapy helps me understand more of the past and my part in the story so far but it is trail running which levers me into the present.

My first night home after running by Loch Rannoch I dream that I am in a corridor with multiple doors along both sides. I rattle door handles, thump on the panelling, feeling distraught and excluded. When I awake I sense the metaphorical corridor is where I need to be for now, to live in the liminal space in-between. I name this dream "The Loch'd Doors" and start imagining where the corridor leads instead. Swiss psychologist Carl Jung described the human journey as containing "two halves of life". There was no questionnaire presented at the time of our conception. We are born into a family story already underway in a certain social, cultural landscape not of our choosing. But as author Julian Barnes says, "the first half of life is inevitable, but the second half can be chosen". The second half of life is not a matter of chronology that clicks in at a certain date like your 40th birthday. The second half is the beginning of a descent back to earth. The second half of life offers an entirely new map by which to navigate the world, but it is a map which emerges as you go along.

But where to run? I print off a map of the United Kingdom and attach it to the bedroom wall. Grabbing a red felt-tip pen I mark fat dots on locations mostly unfamiliar to me: Dartmoor; Snowdon; Cheddar Gorge; the Jurassic Coast; Cambridgeshire Fens; New Forest; covering as much of the map as I can. There are yawning gaps where nothing is marked as if north of Warwickshire is tantamount to visiting the North Pole. (It was another year before I noticed my south-centric bias despite it staring me in the face. Have I been looking southward all these years, magnetised to the familiar? Would the whole configuration of dots on the map change if I included that which I have previously excluded? What else have I not been paying attention to?)

I must trust my feet to feel a way through this liminality. Running a trail marathon each month, between this winter and the next, will be a corridor between the old and new. I scribble a budget on a scrap of paper rescued from the recycling basket. I have time to run, but more importantly I need to recover. It won't be like this forever. It can't be as I have bills to pay. The hurried budget covers all travel costs, race entry fees (where applicable), safety equipment, Ordnance Survey maps, nutrition, and where necessary, accommodation. To pay for the running and travel I refrain from buying a television licence (and from watching TV, obviously), forego alcohol (mostly) and revert to cutting my own hair. I will camp wherever I can. I commit to off-setting my car mileage with tree planting and sign up as a volunteer with a local charity, The Heart of England Forest. Looking at the map I have no idea yet how I will include Northern Ireland in the running plan. I rummage through a bottom drawer to check running kit supplies, holding each item up in turn, like lost property. Most of it is more than a decade old but will suffice. One thing to not skimp on is decent running trainers given the responsibility that feet carry. I buy some Brooks Grit trail shoes which suit my running style and are half price because they are 'last years colours', as if the past is always discounted and only the future has value.

I stand back from the map. It looks like it has caught measles.

But creating possibility also means accepting limitations. There are places where I won't run: Swindon, Norwich, Grimsby and Ayr will have to wait. I create a training spreadsheet which glares from the computer screen, its columns depicting different types of run each in code: tempo, threshold, long, recovery, hill repeats, intervals, pyramids. "Sod this" I mutter, "I'll make it up as I go along...like Coltrane". Trail running and jazz are two dots that have never met before in my brain but instantly fuse. This is not like the Old Days. The future won't be an extension of the past.

I decide on some rules, because when you become a grown up you can invent your own:

Rule No. 1: It doesn't matter how long the process takes, just keep going.

Rule No. 2: ...

I sit quietly considering what Rule No. 2 should be. Nope, one rule is enough. I am more likely to keep it. I decide to use as little technology as possible, opting for a "metric-detox", apart from knowing I've completed the official marathon distance of 26.2 miles. Although I enjoy analysing elevation gained, average pace and VO2 max, eventually numbers numb. My attention needs to be on life out there, not a mini-machine on my wrist. Going off the map means not doing things in the way they've always been done.

Does the distance of running 26.2 miles itself matter? Mileage is just a made-up measure, but the clunky-number of a marathon distance has been a recognised benchmark for over a hundred years. It offers a binary clarity: complete or incomplete? It is a way of saying "okay, that's enough for today". The specific distance also guarantees a decent expanse of time to shake off the entanglements of technology and temperament and tune into what's going on outside my head.

I look up at the map and my hands tremble with excitement. I half expect a knock on my door and a beast with three heads to appear, one for each of my previous school head teachers: Miss Sutton with her heap of coal-black hair, *lanky Mr. Cooper smoking his pipe, and Mr. Leech with his slug-like moustache. "Boy, what are you doing?" the tri-headed beast would grunt, voices echoing through the corridors of time. "Stop dreaming and get on with your work!" My work now is another marathon beginning on my doorstep into a familiar place but at an unfamiliar time.*

THE GEMINIDS

Silence is presence, not absence

The Geminids sounds like an unpleasant condition requiring cream from the doctor. In fact they are an annual meteor shower in mid-December, first discovered in 1862 and named because they appear to radiate from the constellation of Gemini. Over a hundred years later it was discovered that the earth is actually passing through the debris trail of an asteroid. Space litter. The flying sparks are set to peak tonight, at around 2.00 a.m., with up to 80 meteors visible per hour, as Jupiter's gravity pulls the path of debris nearer to earth. Unlike other meteor showers, the Geminids are visible from both northern and southern hemispheres, reaching deeper into the earth's atmosphere, creating long colourful arcs sometimes lasting a couple of seconds. Although stars and meteors don't feature on my red-dotted map of the British Isles, they exist high above it and tonight's conditions are perfect for seeing them.

It is after 10.00 p.m. A My Bloody Valentine record plays, filling the void, its layers of distorted guitar offering music you drown in rather than listen to. If I'm going to run, it has to be now. I hesitate as memories surface of getting mugged at university late one night. Then I remember camping with my children in the New Forest earlier this summer. "Can we stay up and watch shooting stars, Daddy?" my eldest child asked. I was tired, my other children were in their tent asleep. "Let's do it tomorrow" I replied. "But tomorrow might be too late" they said. We looked at each other. I yielded. We dragged a double airbed out of the tent onto the stubbled grass and for the next two hours we lay on our backs, side by side, staring at a sky riddled with starlight, losing count at more than thirty shooting stars. I looked for the "Navigator's Triangle", the three bright stars of Altair, Deneb and Vega (I didn't know their names at the time) which provide direction in the sky. When the Navigator's Triangle rises to its highest point it forms a southward-pointing arrow, a sky-sign saying "You Are Here". I tracked its progress across the sky as if somehow an alignment in the heavens above could re-configure my dismantled life down here, beer can in hand, my body splayed on a sagging airbed. For the remaining time camping, my child was right, the sky was too cloudy to see anything. Sometimes you have to seize the dark.

I lift the needle off the record. A sharp silence frozen in time.

"Life is long if we listen to ourselves often enough, and look up" says Erling Kagge, Norwegian explorer, and the first person to reach the three earthbound poles: North, South and Everest. I'm not yet sure how running in the dark and looking up will work together. The best chance of seeing the meteors, say NASA officials, is to get away from street lights for half an hour to acclimatise to the dark. "Face south", they say "and look at as much of the sky as possible." It is comforting to read that a meteorite "falling all the way to earth is unlikely", although NASA once got fined when debris fell from one of their space stations, landing in Australia.

There is no time to plot a reliable 26.2 mile route. I imagine a constellation of local villages and hamlets: Bidford-on-Avon to Barton, then the long undulating road to Welford, then dash across the main road to Binton; then head out to The Graftons and Exhall, leading to Wixford and Broom, then hopefully return home. If I can't have a map I can see then I need a map I can feel, like Inuit sailors in Greenland who carve coastal maps from lumps of driftwood which they can feel through their fur mittens while travelling in the dark in order to prevent frostbite. Navigation by touch. My feet will have to be the guide.

I cover my toes with petroleum jelly, still severely blistered from a day-long run of 30 (very slow) miles three weeks before to Broadway Tower and around the Cotswolds to retain stamina from the Loch Rannoch run. (It was a while before I realised how damaging mineral hydrocarbons in petroleum jelly are to both human body and the environment as a by-product of oil production. It was an old habit, a reference point in the routine, one which changed as time went on). Into the rucksack goes a flask of hot blackcurrant squash and an under-ripe banana. Click-click. Click-click. Damn. The head torch batteries are flat. It will be a darker journey than anticipated. With reflective fluorescent straps around each calf and bicep, I leap down four flights of stairs to the ground floor. The door creaks open and the cold slap of night hits. The door clicks shut. I feel alone. It strikes me that I have this freedom, this assumption of reasonable safety as a man in a way not always available for women, as if personal safety were a gender entitlement. It's another thing I'd never considered. Another dot hiding in my blindspot.

Crossing the village stone bridge built by monks 600 years ago, my body jolts in search of rhythm. Streetlights hold vigil at the village boundary then it is just darkness as I run along Buckle Street, the old Roman road. Grey clouds dissipate, like pencil smudges being erased, revealing a velvet-dark hole. Dabs of stars emerge looking like splinters of ice. How many nights have I driven in haste ignoring all this that blinks from above? It takes time for sight to adapt to the new dark, about half an hour, but once adapted, night vision becomes a heightened sense, navigating by shadows not objects, entering territory of more uncertainty not less. Visual boundaries of self blur into the darkspace which contains you. You become the night.

As I run, I consider whether running a marathon alone through the night is a sane choice. The psychological chaos of the previous year is still raw and not much feels settled or stable although I have set up my own business and am working three days a week. The moon illuminates my steps beyond the village boundary. Moonlight and mental health have a long-standing association. Our word "lunatic" comes from luna, the Latin for moon, because the moon phases were once thought to be the cause of insanity. Greek philosopher Aristotle argued a full moon caused what we now call Bipolar Disorder because increased moonlight disturbed people's sleep. Until as recently as the 1960s, "lunatic" remained the dominant legal term in the UK to define people experiencing mental illness, before the mental asylums closed.

The trauma of significant loss can trigger unpredictable changes in personality as the severe impact of shock can increase the risk of psychosis, to which a person may already have a genetic predisposition. Psychosis is an experience not a clinical diagnosis, affecting about 1 in 100 adults at any point in time. It is not a static condition but often an "episode" which typically passes when conditions of relational and environmental distress lessen. Psychosis is when perception of reality, mood and behaviour are significantly disrupted, and thinking moves non-linearly, like a knight piece in chess. Ideas become odd, rather than creative. Having "special" information or "being on a mission" directed by outside forces, hearing audible voices or having hallucinations all indicate the presence of psychosis to some degree. Inevitably it will be worsened (or triggered) by using hallucinogenic drugs, especially cannabis. We can relate to how psychosis feels through our less troubling experiences of half-remembered dreams (what's real? what isn't?), extreme tiredness or flu (when you don't feel "with it"), the warped perception when looking at things under water, and that sense of life not being coherent, solid or structured. Whereas Bipolar Disorder includes both extremes of manic highs with obsessive fixations then bouts of low mood and depression, psychosis does not have this swing-effect. Rather than labelling people "psychotic" (which doesn't help anyone), we need to understand something significant has happened or is happening to them. We may not be best-placed to support them personally, but we can listen with an aim to understand. Understanding from a place of compassion dissipates stigma and supports someone being able to access appropriate help. When the trauma of loss is kept secret it festers, possibly deepening a sense of shame ("is there something wrong with me?"), guilt ("is this my fault?"), and fear ("what will happen to me?"). These are powerful mental states, embedded neurologically and biologically, and can trigger harm to oneself and others. We have to talk and understand more about the complex human experience, especially states of distress and their impact, rather than reverting to judgement and blame which are defensive reactions used to avoid connection. To listen and understand is to love. And love is always the biggest risk we take.

During my months of living in the "shed" I spoke to a friend, Linda, an experienced therapist and an expert in working with people experiencing psychosis and PTSD (post-traumatic stress disorder). I was familiar with talking about these conditions with others through my training but I couldn't recognise they were part of my own experience. The self can't see itself anymore than your nose can smell itself or your tongue taste itself. We need other people as mirrors, as eyes and ears to say truthfully what they see and hear, otherwise we become locked-in by blindspots and false assumptions.

Hearing voices was the scariest thing, "auditory hallucinations", audible sentences next to my head causing me to spin around to see who was there, but seeing no one. I saw things in my dreams which showed up in reality the next day, like a specific car registration number or a persons face. I felt frightened that the boundary between sleeping and waking suddenly felt permeable. That year, in my journal, I wrote down over 200 night-dreams as my unconscious mind became overwhelmed with symbolic noise. Three times I experienced out of body sensations, including once when I fell through darkness for several minutes before landing what felt like an inch above the carpet, before an audible voice said "there is only light". It wasn't a dream because I was awake when it happened. It was terrifying, like being unplugged from the Rational Brain Mainframe. Of course it feels vulnerable leaving these sentences on the page for others to mock. I understand that. They have kept me awake at night. Perhaps I shouldn't admit to the depression, and definitely not to the episode of psychosis? Will I lose credibility as a result? Will people trust me less or think I am damaged goods? Is it unprofessional? All emotion is data and wants to reveal something. I finally clocked the parallel of how I felt about translating my experience to these pages with how others can feel in opening up about their experiences of grief, distress and transcendence. I wrote, edited, deleted, rewrote, on and on. But then I heard my uncle yelling in my memory, "leave it all on the road!" I can write these words because I have come out the other side alive. There are years of distance between then and now. But there was a long time I never thought I would. How will we ever dismantle the stigma that contributes to people taking their own life unless we speak the truth of our experience? "It's not that there's something wrong with you" Linda affirmed, her vivid red lipstick imprinting itself on the lip of the coffee cup, "it's about what has happened to you. This is the grieving you, the trying to-cope version of you." That sentence, spoken with the gravity of compassion in a safe environment where I could risk saying "help!" was a lifeline. Her empathy and counsel settled something in my central nervous system, helped me feel the ground again.

    PTSD is also common after a traumatic experience, often including symptoms of physical nausea, sweating, eruptions of panic and sudden mental flashbacks (sometimes several minutes long, as if in a trance). The person goes into a state of hyper-vigilance of always expecting something bad to happen, alert to every micro-sound and movement in the environment - the slam of a door, a raised voice. These are common symptoms and yet each person's experience will be unique to them, like a signature response. Studies have shown that when PTSD is occurring, the body carries on releasing the stress hormones cortisol and adrenaline as if preparing it for a threat, even when the threat has Adrenaline passes within minutes, but cortisol levels can d for months impairing physical hearing. Self-harming and ation often become common, a high-risk attempt to get rid of the pain, as if trying to make the emotion visible. Complex PTSD can occur when someone is harmed by someone close to them they trusted (betrayal is a common cause) or when experiencing multiple traumas and/or losses together. Reading words about all this on a page will do nothing to prepare you for the direct, visceral experience of feeling constantly trapped, crushed, ashamed and petrified.

Linda helped me match cause and effect and develop grounding practices (like pressing my heels into the ground and regulating my breathing). I recognise now that it took two years for the hyper-vigilance to completely settle. To not freak out when I came across a locked door, heard certain names in conversation, saw certain cars, as if the past was resurrecting itself in the present, pushing old panic buttons in my brain. The darkness of those heightened liminal years were terrifying and "lunatic" was a word that may have described how I felt on the inside. But things change. Blame becomes a source of enquiry, and truths get spoken without the need to stir up old drama. Truth does its own work, in its own time.

Despite the pitch darkness this is a familiar road. I ran this way yesterday afternoon passing a dozen grounded gliders in a field, their wingtips leaning upon the earth like work-weary folk at the bar. Above them a flurry of fieldfares darted and dived with tireless delight, flashing black and white, sounding like sky-laughter. Birdsong has long been a source of what environmental psychologists call "soft fascination", like contemplating cloud-drift or the sunrise, offering a focus for meditation. The calming effect of certain nature sounds, like birdsong or trickling water, may be down to our evolution, indicating an environment already abundant with resources where we may be safer, so we can settle. Tuning into pleasant, natural sounds offers a break from the relentless wheel of internal dialogue which can be exhausting if those thoughts are anxious, compulsive or depressing. The British Natural History Museum found that during the first coronavirus lockdown in Spring 2020, nearly three-quarters of people in the UK reported hearing louder bird song, due to less traffic and human noise. Birdsong can jolt us out of the solitary confinement of ruminating thoughts and into what philosopher Alan Watts described as "the hum and buzz of the world". Many classical composers have been inspired by birdsong: Beethoven's Pastoral Symphony mimicked the quail, cuckoo and nightingale, Mozart listened to a starling for inspiration, and the great tit features in Bruckner's fourth symphony. However, none rival Olivier Messiaen who travelled across France for fifty years, sleeping in the wild, risking his life to translate the contours of birdsong into visible maps of crotchets, quavers, semi-quavers. For Messiaen, birdsong was a direct link to heaven.

It is easy for our attention to become anchored downward toward the computer keyboard, desk, pavement, plate, or phone. When we're not looking down, our attention is usually straight ahead at the road, person, canvas, corridor or screen before us. Gazing up can feel alien, forgetting life happens up there too. Recently my father, a keen bird watcher, looked up from his front garden in South Warwickshire when, for the first time in his life, he spotted a sea eagle high on the thermals, on its way to the Yorkshire moors. Neurologist Oliver Sacks, towards the end of his life, recommended that instead of trying to understand the large problems of how we humans think, we should just sit alone, under stars, gazing at them (not necessarily on an air bed). A mutual gaze of looking out and looking in, as if seeing through both ends of a telescope at the same time.

Tonight's sky is prolific with stars. Old constellations flicker as if sending a message down the corridor of time. Instead of fieldfares flashing I see the ever-silent constellation of Orion, whose name means "rising in the sky" or "dawning". Orion has been around a while, described by Homer nearly three thousand years ago as "a tall hunter, armed with an unbreakable bronze club" and by Greek astronomer Ptolemy as "having a lion's pelt". Orion certainly wants to be taken seriously (maybe that's why it is my favourite constellation). I spot the three bright stars of Orion's belt and then the three stars of his dagger dangling from the belt. The dagger is like a needle on a gauge: on the left it points eastward, vertically down is south and to the right points west, the angle of the dagger changing relative to the horizon.

Peering through the window of The Bell Inn pub at Welford, seven miles into the run, last orders have long since passed. Pint glasses stand drained on the bar, the room void of life. I cross the main road and the stars suddenly blink shut overhead. The air feels ancient and thick with death, as if I am running through an unseen substance. My body shivers. St. Peter's Church graveyard is screened by a tunnel of mature beech trees, separating me from starlight, their corkscrewed trunks resembling something from a Brothers Grimm fairytale. I remember a friend's funeral earlier this week. Alan was the funniest, most quirky man I ever knew. A short, mathematical genius from the island of Mauritius. He was Best Man at my wedding, where he composed a song with my brother about my haircut looking like the cartoon character Tintin. Once, volunteering with him, visiting people living on the streets in Wandsworth, Alan got out of the van he had hired (full of flasks of soup, blankets, second hand sleeping bags and so on), and the van keys fell out of his hand down the roadside drain. He looked down, then looked at me. "What a gutter!" he said and then laughed for ages at the irony of his own joke. "But what about the keys?" I asked, peering down the drain trying to retrieve them. He shrugged and laughed again, "What a gutter!" Alan was diagnosed with pancreatic cancer at the age of 54 and died within six weeks. His wife told me that Alan saw angels just before he died. Perhaps they had finally retrieved the keys from the drain. Tears are on my face as I run, past dozens of gangly rowans leaning in from both sides of the road. It is as dark as night gets. There are no shadows, only cold space to run through. I quicken my pace.

The road inclines another mile toward The Blue Boar pub whose lights are also out, the car park as lifeless as the graveyard. I turn right at a cross-roads, then stop in a lay-by and wriggle free of the backpack. The flask clinks on cold stones and the moon illuminates gravel at my feet. Except for the sound of pouring hot squash into a mug it is silent.

I watch the steam rise, white hieroglyphics dancing their way to meet the stars, mingling with my breath, wavering like a ghost. Two meteors streak down, from top-left and top-right toward each other, their trails creating an impression of two hands on a clock meeting at the centre, suggesting it is ten minutes to 2.00 a.m.

"To speak is precisely what the silence should do. It should speak and you should talk with it" says explorer Erling Kagge. "A great many of us have a desire to return to something basic, authentic, to find peace; to experience a small, quiet alternative to the din" he says. Silence conjures up abstract ideas of a dark vacuum into which we might be sucked, the words "silence" and "awkward" often not far apart in speech. We consider silence as either absence - what remains after removing all noise - or as an oppression needing to be broken by an authoritative voice, a notification on the phone, an idea, command or BREAKING NEWS. Relief arrives because the silence is over and something is happening we can describe, point at, react to, share, obey, argue with, control or do. If silence is perceived as an enemy, it becomes inevitable that we lurch back into a matrix of noise. In Latin, "noise" links to our words "nausea" (from seasickness because those suffering didn't stay quiet) and "noxious" (from the noise of quarrels). But silence is presence, not absence. Silence is remedy for a noisy mind, a moment of appreciating everything that has gone, and the anticipation of everything yet to emerge. There is a quality of grace to silence.

A lorry belches past on the A46 causing the ground to shake under its clanking weight, a temporary intrusion until quiet returns.

Many creation stories (Babylonian, Egyptian, Judeo-Christian and Norse) all say silence was the beginning of all things. The word "silence" comes from both an old Gothic verb anasilan meaning "the wind dies down", and the Latin desinere, a word meaning "stop". Silence is not vacancy, but present stillness, and "stillness", says spiritual teacher Eckhart Tolle "is intelligence". Silence is not a dangerous thing out there we have to track and trace in order to avoid it, but a foundation upon which all life rests. Silence can be a sanctuary where the mental winds "die down" and our chattering thoughts stop. Silence is 24/7 help. It untwists, untangles. In silence we can come back to our breath, the thrum of our beating heart, blinking eyes, the automatic processes of the reptilian brain. We can notice the gaps between breaths, the fleeting liminal spaces that help life make sense and give it continuity, like semibreve or fermata rests in music. We can drop from the analytical mind to a deeper place, tuning in once more to life's ordinary soundtrack: Bleeps. Clicks. Taps. Thumps. Thuds. Slams. Coughs. The suction noise of the fridge. Clanking bottles. Water gushing from a tap. Gravel crunching. Scrapes. Pings. Sighs. Birdsong. All sound originates from silence. Sounds are sounds, there's no hierarchy to them. Like all sensations, they are free of thinking. This very moment we can notice how silence hides between, beneath and behind each sound, always there, a unique continuity between moments and months, eras and eons. Silence is "the new luxury" says Kagge. Silence beckons us to slow down, to surrender to the flow of life and truly listen to what's happening. To be fully here. "If you're always talking to yourself in your head" said philosopher Alan Watts, "how on earth can you listen to the real world?"

Here, beneath the intense starlight, the presence of interior silence formed from two hours of running alone, feels like contentment. A Geminid meteor strikes out across a panther-skin sky, an explosive curl of light, stealing my breath, causing a pause.

Silence has tone and grade, it is weight without words. It is neither manufactured, nor the property of any ideology. It arises from within every one of us, much the same way as plums are not stuck onto a plum tree, but emerge from the very life of the thing itself. Silence belongs to us all, holds and includes us all, knits us together in a shared environment. Under this vast night sky, I wonder what type of silence this is. Around 50 years ago, playwright and psychotherapist Paul Goodman examined what he identified as nine types of silence we might encounter. Goodman mused about "the dumb silence of slumber" and the "fertile silence of awareness, pastoring the soul, whence emerge new thoughts; the alive silence of alert perception, ready to say, 'This...

this…'" He suggests there is a silence which is "sober", one that is "musical", another which is "noisy" (like resentment), or the "silence of listening to another speak, catching the drift and helping him be clear". But in this moment, beneath the colour-arcs of the Geminids, it is another type of silence he offers which I relate to, "the silence of peaceful accord with other persons or communion with the cosmos."

Another lorry drums pasts, its two white beams scouring the road to find its way. I listen as it scurries down the hill, its volume shrinking as if slurped into a black hole. In the temporary absence of traffic, silence returns from temporary hiding. I look up at the star-scattered sky, tiny pinpricks crescendoing with light, an orchestral dot-to-dot humming with unity. Somehow this nearly nothing feels like everything. What I hear is silence, and what I see are stars, but what I feel (apart from cold toes) is wonder. Humans can launch satellites, perform brain surgery, transfer images from one side of the planet to another with a click, but could we ever measure wonder? Or for that matter, could we measure gratitude, mystery, awe, clarity, instinct, empathy, compassion, grace? The wonder of life is immeasurable.

In the centre of my line of sight I watch a slow moving yellow scratch, the longest meteor I see tonight, emerging then fading. I stand for a while, chin arrowed to the sky. Between spiralling white breaths, I count eleven shooting stars, each falling like drops of mercury into oblivion. It sparks a memory: One night, last winter, around midnight, I noticed through the window it was snowing. I dragged on a coat over my pyjamas, slipped on an old pair of trainers and walked a mile to the edge of the village where the streetlights extinguished. I stood, face surrendered to the sky, watching snowflakes tumbling like ash falling, white squares escaping from an infinite black hole, landing upon my eyelids, dissolving upon my lips, receiving them like mercy.

Silence, it seems, is a condition for contentment. A chance to hear yourself think, and to hear yourself not thinking quite so much, allowing the mind to return to what philosopher John Locke described as "blank paper mode": the mind's natural state upon which nature and experience inscribes its own impressions.

I lift my backpack from the gravel and slide it onto my shoulders. Gravel crunches underfoot. I exhale, breath appearing like a dust cloud. Turning towards the village of Temple Grafton the grass verges have become varnished in frost and in the moonlight the road has the sheen of a thin bridal veil, testament to the clarity of the night. I feel my way in the dark, down thin lanes I don't know, feeling lost. Several times there is a crashing flap from shadowed trees, my movement disturbing a bird trying to sleep. A barn owl swoops in front of me, a white ghost exploding its wings open against a black sky. I turn onto a narrow track into the hamlet of Bickmarsh and look at my watch: I have run 19.2 miles. I run a while longer, legs as rigid as stilts and fingers numb, despite two pairs of gloves. I long for bed. I check the watch again: 19.9 miles. Everything unwinds in slow motion. Continuing happens without speech, music, thought or drama.

It is past 3.00 a.m. when the watch battery dies. The phone battery indicates 1%. I shut it down. All measurement and false light are gone. I have been running for nearly five hours (I won't know until tomorrow when I retrace the route that I complete a marathon distance by 0.2 miles). I look up. Everything has moved by degrees since I began. "The starry sky is the truest friend in life" says Kagge, "it is ever there", a reminder "that your restlessness, your doubt, your pains are passing trivialities". There isn't any falling debris from a space station, so that's something for which to be thankful. Orion still chases the Seven Sisters, but my hunting for the night is done. I head home.

The street lights in the village are off as I stagger to the front door, slip key into lock, and look one last time at Orion's triple star-studded belt. Three stars hanging out together, like silence, stillness, wonder. Unlocking the front door of the flat cold air hits my face. The boiler has broken. A breath swirls like a genie wanting to grant a wish. I could wish to not ache, or for a boiler which works, but my wish has been granted because I watched breath, stars and meteors rise and fall upon a sky-canvas, renewing an appreciation for the long-span of time, remembering life is a temporary flicker in a still-exploding cosmos, a song being composed, a tiny dot on a big map still in the process of creation.

    I tumble into sleep having added a dot right where I live, a kind of homecoming. The next dot is the other side of New Years Eve, beckoning me back to a place of memory.

HAYLING ISLAND

What you seek is reconciliation with yourself

Bleep-Bleep. I cover my ears with the duvet but it's no use. Thoughts of hot sand, picnics and salty air fill my mind. Bleep-Bleep. Nostalgia keeps me awake, that longing for another time rather than another place, aided by the intermittent bleeping of the smoke alarm on the landing outside the front door. Bleep-Bleep. Muttering expletives, I manoeuvre from the bed to the hallway like an undercover agent, feeling a way in the dark. Rummaging for a screwdriver, a hammer falls from the shelf landing next to my toes. Annoyance turns to relief. The alarm, I soon discover, is wired in to the main system of the whole block of flats, so I can't fix it without outside help. The brain-pattern repeats: sand, picnics, salty air, electronic bleeping.

At 5.00 a.m. I tip out of bed for the second time, hold a mug of black coffee which steams as I stare at the map of measles on the bedroom wall. Two dots have turned red to blue: a solitary blue dot in the throat of Scotland and one at the heart of the map. There is a long way to go, but each dot bulges with possibility. Today is about a red dot perched above the Isle of Wight, throbbing like a sore toe.

Hayling Island dangles like an upside-down letter 'T' off the county of Hampshire on England's southern coast. Islands have boundaries you can't easily dispute. You know when you are either on or off them, where they begin and end, unlike memory or family history. I played on South Hayling beach as a child: the blistering hotness of sand between toes, the curved grass hump between beach and car park looking like a solid wave you could surf upon. Ascension on pause. It is 40 years since I have been there.

As I drive, sky lightens from heron-grey to the white of new paper, the South Down chalk-banks channelling me towards today's running haven, down, down, ready to slide off the mainland onto Hayling Island and disappear, like a snooker cue ball into a pocket.

Parking at the Hayling Island Amateur Dramatic (HIAD) Society requires just a twenty metre walk to the race start line. The Station Theatre, where the HIAD Society is based, used to be the goods shed for the Hayling Billy Line, the island railway which ran between here and Havant for around a century, before finally closing in 1962. Hundreds of visitors came here each summertime, crammed in small locomotives to enjoy the beach, but on too many winter days, like today, too few visitors came to make the railway economically sustainable. Since the closure of the railway nearly 60 years ago it has become a local nature reserve, flush with wading birds including Redshanks, Shelducks, Oyster Catchers with their carrot stick beaks, and Grey Plovers.

Walking to the start line there are puddles which have more blue sky reflected in them than seems possible on such an overcast day. The race registration desk sits under a gazebo trembling in the wind next to a table laden with sausage rolls, pretzels and cheese cubes. A feast worthy of a locomotive trip, surely. A commanding voice pierces the conversations of the runners. "If you want to use the toilets" the race director announces to anyone listening, "you'll have to go someplace else. Our portaloos were vandalised last night". He points toward two sad Tardis-looking specimens, recently resurrected from their fall. I soon discover their interior is decorated with mounds of wet toilet tissue like limpets on a rock. "The toilet chemicals are spilled over there", he continues, pointing towards the car park I've just walked through where blue-dyed ethanol soaks the Tarmac, explaining the apparent overdose of skylight in the puddles.

Running "laps of the island" was never mentioned in the event marketing, it was just my assumption. There is nothing circular about this race, which I should have realised by the shape of the island. "Nah mate" a tall Ed Sheeran lookalike tells me upon my questioning, "it's just two and a bit miles up this old railway track, okay, yeah", he nods slowly, his fringe waving at me to check if I am ready for the climax, "and then you just run back again. Yeah? That IS the lap, mate." He glances up the track, then turns back to look me in the eye. "It is really dull", he laughs, shoulders quivering. There is no danger of over-selling this run.

I return to the car, slump in the driver seat and do the sums: To complete the marathon distance will require six runs up and six back down the same disused railway line. The car windscreen fogs up as I pour black tea from the flask. Resting the mug on my knee I feel a surge of warmth. "It's okay", I reassure myself, "today can be training for the Dartmoor trail marathon next month". Except Dartmoor will be undulating and strenuous, bounding across a marshy expanse under the eye of ancient Tors studded across the moor, navigating one of the few remaining wild places in Britain. Today's course is flat, repetitive and as appealing as the interior of a pole-axed portaloo.

The race director gives final instructions based on "don't run too far down the track and get lost" which stirs the temptation to do precisely that. There are about sixty runners, most shivering or pogo-ing on the spot to keep warm, faces half-covered with a buff neck-scarf. In little more than a year such face coverings will become a mandatory part of daily life in shops, schools and on public transport but on this dull pre-pandemic morning, people are just trying to keep warmth in, rather than disease out. I stand at the rear by the bright blue puddles. A whistle blows, the group moves, dozens of running devices bleep-bleeping so as the marathon begins I think about a faulty smoke alarm, a hammer landing by my toes and a red dot on a map. I want to hit STOP but something urges me on.

Storm-stunted oaks form a tunnel through which we run, warty branches twisted together like witch fingers. A line of trees perpendicular to the harbour's west shore have been briskly brushed back by wind, west to east, appearing like a ramp ascending from the water so the trees look shocked, as if their roots are plugged into an electric socket deep underground. Elemental forces of nature, invisible acting upon visible, transient upon solid, wind upon wood, music captured in arboreal form.

Half a mile along the path, a view opens up across Langstone Harbour: grey water confronting a chalk-white sky, as if the day is hungry for the infiltration of colour. A wooden signpost indicates "Saltmarshes" are a mile inland and oyster banks, fished in the harbour since Roman times, are just ahead. Salt was a vital source of trade on the island from the 11th century continuing for around 800 years. As sea levels rise, saltmarsh survives by migrating further inland, in constant retreat seeking a new home. A natural refugee. The salt-scent reminds me of picnics on the beach as a child, a temporary home for the afternoon, like sitting on the edge of a map gazing at long-off horizons.

The running route flirts with the harbour shore, small pink flags spiked along the path indicating the way. I'm supposed to be running a marathon but I've veered off track, place becoming more important than pace. Venturing onto the beach, pebbles crunch beneath trainers like the sound of eating crisps with your mouth open. Waves finger a path between sea beet and sea kale, old fishing line and disheveled plastic bottles. The incoming tide pokes the litter as if to say "you shouldn't be here, please leave". In six months time golden samphire will flower here, a plant that can smell like shoe polish. Somewhere beneath the waves are diminishing numbers of cuttlefish, pipefish and spiny seahorses. Wooden poles driven into the beach as a coastal defence have been knocked apart like bowled cricket stumps. The untidiness seems a temporary truce between sea and shore. A contested place.

Beyond an upturned rowing boat in someone's front garden, the first turning point appears. I twist through the metal gate, the track curving toward the beach. Wind shoves me back like a bully against a wall. A cluster of ringed plovers sweep across the bay, playful and fast, scything over the heads of parading Brent geese as two runners talk ahead of me. "I can't be doing with the speed anymore" I hear one say, discussing motivation, I assume, rather than Class B drugs. "Did you enjoy it?" a man in his late fifties replies, "that's what I always ask runners first, not what their time was, but did you enjoy the damn thing?"

Returning to the start line gazebo, I collect a pink elastic band and ping it over my wrist marking one lap completed, then scoop a handful of salt-crested pretzels. The positive thing about running 2.2 miles up then back each way, six times over, means the turning points come thick and fast which might be easier psychologically than running a 26.2 mile circuit.

On the second lap my mind turns to vinyl records I bought in my teenage years. Sifting through images of Pet Shop Boys and Paul McCartney on 7" paper squares, another image surfaces, forgotten for 30 years: an hour glass on a black record sleeve, golden sand flowing in reverse, upward from present to past. "The Living Years" by Mike and The Mechanics was released in 1989, a song about the regret of unspoken words to a father, a desire to repair the past, and the full circle of life with the birth of a child. I remember as a fifteen year old kneeling on the bedroom carpet before leaving for school, gripping the hourglass-image record sleeve, flipping it over and over, trying to reverse the flow of sand so it ran from the past back to the present, a metaphor for what I am doing now as I run.

Relationships are the main context in which we are hurt and therefore are the main context in which we heal. Our early relationships shape the neural map by which we navigate the rest of our life. Psychologist John Bowlby was noted for his research 50 years ago into attachments, suggesting that all children, from birth, need to develop a strong, supportive relationship with at least one primary caregiver for the child to develop socially and emotionally. "Attachment is a deep and enduring emotional bond" said Bowlby, "that connects one person to another across time and space". The attachments we make (or fail to make) create templates for all our future relationships.

Healthy attachments provide an unconditional sense of security, a feeling of "I'm truly safe with this person", resulting from consistent emotional responses where the other person "tunes in" to your emotions and is able to name feelings, "you sound cross" or "you look sad". You feel at ease in your body, you don't have to force things. Secure attachments help create positive internal dialogue: "People will help me; my needs will be responded to; I deserve care and concern; the world is mostly friendly". Healthy attachments activate oxytocin, the neurochemical which gives the feeling of care and acceptance, not just with people, but with the natural world too. This is the "chemistry" we feel when we bond with someone or somewhere. Secure attachments aren't only about physical presence (who is there), but emotional attunement (who listens and understands) and are a vital source of resilience, "a lifelong gift" said pioneering neuroscientist Jaak Panksepp, supporting the ability to ask for help without shame or embarrassment. The reluctance to ask for help in adult life can often be traced back to a deficit in early life attachments.

We find attachment clues about our own lives in the photographs and souvenirs we keep, and the places to which we return. *Why that object? Who gave it to you? Where is it from? What's special about that place? What feelings does it evoke?* What seems like random objects to others find their place in a skein of personal meaning.

We all need a safe base early in life as a starting point to feel like we belong on life's mainland, but nobody escapes childhood unscathed. Most of us experience psychological dislocations at some point causing us to question to whom and what we belong, perhaps from difficulties at school, in the family home, bereavements, conflicts. This is the stuff of life, but traumatic experiences can create deep deficits of love, acceptance and attention. Insecure attachments then cause us to perceive absence rather than presence and be hypersensitive to threat rather than detect actual safety: "People will be angry with me; others frighten me; I don't deserve care; I need others to validate me; I must be on my guard; the world is a scary place". These messages often sit just beneath our conscious thinking, only becoming apparent when we over-react and we wonder "where the heck did that reaction come from?" We cannot see the lens through which we experience the world without accurate feedback from others.

It was Linda who reminded me that attachment isn't only toward others, but also to the physical places where we are and to the body we inhabit. Attachment isn't just a psychological construct or theory we can bash about in conversation. We experience attachment through our physical senses, body responses (tension being an indicator) and breathing, which collectively are our most reliable anchors to the present. When old traumas get activated (often in the context of the family but also in the workplace) we stop being in the here-and-now because we are yanked back to there-and-then. As Panksepp's research into the emotional systems in the brain shows, our fear, rage and panic systems become magnified, blocking our cognitive ability to care for ourselves, depleting our initiative to seek help or form positive attachments and shrinking our perspective. Ease recedes as the body tightens, throat constricts, voice tone thins. We regress from a stable adult state (if that was available) where we can be enquiring, robust and compassionate to a distraught childlike state where our options become limited, less mature, more reactive. In Linda's words, "there's not something wrong with you, but something significant is happening - or has happened - to you." Exploring and understanding our own attachment patterns more clearly gives us a wider range of responses when the old stuff revs into action.

Empathy, which leads to compassion, is key. Feel it, communicate it. The presence of empathy in a relationship literally changes the brain's neural structure by promoting the development of pathways in the frontal lobes, calming the brain's alarm system. Receiving empathy quietens the internal BLEEP-BLEEP messages which have been busy perceiving threat. Empathy enables us to think more coherently because the body can sense greater safety. But we can't do Speed Empathy, like Speed Dating. Empathy requires slowing down to notice other people's facial expressions, voice tones, eye movements, the words they say and the words they don't say. Rather than assuming we know what others experience, we can use phrases like "I wonder...(if you're feeling scared?)", "I notice...(that you sound tired)", "I imagine...(this is hard for you right now)". Receiving empathic attention reconnects us with our immediate physical experience and inner strength, which becomes a source of felt-safety, restoring connection with others. When we experience empathy "the whole feel of the world changes" said Panksepp. This is what good therapy provides and why I encourage people to be open to it. The brain's chemical systems (opioids, oxytocin, prolactin) which conjure the subtle feelings we describe as acceptance, nurture and warmth become dominant in the brain. Empathy re-establishes our internal equilibrium, enabling us to re-attach to ourselves, to the present moment, to the ground we stand on. Empathy heals, then compassion creates.

Langstone Harbour opens out to the right as I return down the Hayling Billy Line. Feet scuff the track, tiny explosions of dust rising and settling in new patterns. Adjacent to the path is a strange, curved concrete slab, a larger-than-life sculpture of a little tern, one of the nature reserve residents. The solid bird has its wings clapped together, as if in prayer. In this position, the bird looks like a windsurfer, its wings as the sail, body as the board, an inverted T-shape just like the island it calls home. It was in Langstone Harbour a few years before the railway line closed that windsurfing was invented by Peter Chilvers as a 12 year old boy experimenting with a sail and a board. Hayling Island hums with origins: along with Chilvers' invention of windsurfing, there's a timber shrine from the Iron Age, around the 1st century, excavated from beneath farmland in the late 1970s; and the most ancient yew tree in the country has its roots here, boasting a nine-metre girth (in fact, its trunk and branches are here too, thankfully, all connected). It seems apt to be running on the first Sunday of the year which is also Epiphany. Hints of beginnings, gifts, origins.

A thrashing movement in the hedgerow wrenches my attention from the path. A plastic supermarket bag, torn and tangled upon thorns flaps like a distressed bird, along with remnants of a dozen burst blue balloons which at first I mistake for discarded surgeons gloves. Litter has been chucked here, a ticking time-bomb of pollution. Fizzy drink cans lay crushed like roadkill beneath the hedge. A stream is dammed with crisp packets, infested with barcode stripes and customer helpline numbers. Someone enjoyed a party here recently and used nature as the trash can. We can remain blind to the sheer volume of litter choking our natural habitats when speeding by in vehicles, but on foot when we travel not only slower but also nearer to what we truly inhabit, dissolving the touchlessness of daily life, we witness what Roger Deakin called "the unmistakeable skullduggery" of what we inflict on our natural home.

On the fourth lap I notice a circle of withered oaks obscuring the harbour view. In the clearing a child sits upon a rope swing, swaying in metronomic movement. "Hurry up, come on, I haven't got all day" yells a man, hunched in a black jacket, who I assume to be the child's father. Pre-loaded parental phrases I have heard myself repeat too many times, as if someone is pulling a string in my back, a programmed voice on repeat. I remember the menu of messages in childhood from authority figures: "Hurry up. Be nice. Play fair. Try hard. Be strong. Get it right." I am not sure those internalised messages work as well in adulthood. There comes a time when we must put those introjected childhood messages away and replace them with a more compassionate and realistic narrative. The child on the swing, like a symbol of contemplation, gazes across the harbour, ignoring the father's chastisement, lost in the momentum of the swing. I follow the line of his gaze to a power station on the other side, protruding from the horizon like an angry red hand, its chimney smoking with fury and rising into the sky like an erect middle finger.

Four laps run. 17.6 miles. I snap another elastic band onto my wrist then claim a sausage roll and cube of cheese as a reward. Runners' feet slip-slap upon the old railway path, disturbing puddles, leaving trainer-grid impressions upon the mud. I kick up oak leaves, their texture like shredded brown paper bags, swirling, detached from the safety of the earth where they had rested. "This is what I came here for," I think, "to begin again." To find where the boundary of this new self might be lurking. As runners we are littered up and down the track, conversations happening in staccato, energy stored for the final miles to come. The old railway line has become an avenue of serenity. There is nothing grandiose here. It is a simple place.

A runner passes me in the other direction, smiling. "Twenty miles run and you're still bloody smiling?" I want to say. His face is perfectly round like a paper plate. It's one of those generous smiles, more than politeness, a smile which knows it belongs to that face. He has been smiling the entire run. I never learn his name, trade or personal history, but his smile is energising and I cannot help but smile back each time I see him, mirror neurons in action. De-coding his smile, it suggests "Be here, be happy". A quiet permission to let go of former things and drop into the moment. For the first time, I see how in small ways this island shaped me: childhood days playing on the beach here being the origin for a lifelong love of coasts, an apprenticeship for gazing across water. I look across the harbour, each wave carrying a tiny white hat of froth as if coming up for air before plunging back into its larger self.

I steady myself for the final up-and-back lap. Kieran, the race director, comes over and tells me there is time for a seventh lap too "if you hurry". There is an urgency in his tone and fire in his eyes like a visionary seeing things far off. I sigh, my shoulders slump. My body only has fuel for one more lap and it's time I listen to my body rather than my ego.

As I approach the metal gate before the final turning point, a dark mass launches into the sky as if by detonation. A storm cloud of a hundred geese twist, smoke-like, then plummet, piercing the harbour skin like bullets. Their connectivity triggers something in me, a chain reaction of energy, so as I make the final turn, having run more than 24 miles, I begin sprinting, arms pumping, mouth grunting. "Yes! Let's do this!" I hear myself say. It feels like a sprint but I look like a drunken man groping for the bar. I reach the finish line gazebo having run for just short of five hours. Six elastic bands, most of them pink, hang from my wrist as proof. As per the race protocol, I grasp the handbell from the trestle table of cheese cubes and shake it vigorously to indicate "It is finished". Kieran places a medal the size of a donut over my head, then hugs me. Then I remember my secret reward: a pork pie stashed in the boot of the car. I hobble across the car park disturbing the blue puddles by the resurrected portaloos, so the sky seems to expand at my feet.

In the car, pork pie crumbs fall from my fingers onto the horizontal lines of the book bought in Pitlochry, "Walden" by Henry David Thoreau, a book I have thumbed in numerous bookshops over the years, as if waiting to grow up before purchasing a copy. "Could a greater miracle take place" says Thoreau, "than for us to look through each other's eyes for an instant?". Looking through the eyes of my child-self, last here 40 years ago, what would he make of this adult-self with potency and autonomy? Reversing the car out of the car park, I decide to visit South Hayling beach again. Driving through vacant streets, past a closed fish and chip shop, I see the grass-ridge, the wave frozen in time leading onto the beach just as I remember it. The sandy beach has been replaced by shingle dredged from the Solent sea floor to help prevent flooding and erosion, but four decade old memories remain in tact.

Even on a January afternoon, I sense in my imagination the hotness of the sand and salty air.

Through the half-open car window I stare at the shingle and like a cinematic projection from my mind, I look through the eyes of my four year old self, smallest in the family, often loitering at the edge of the family photo. I imagine him wearing his favourite t-shirt, the one with the words "The Rescuers" on it from a Disney cartoon of that era. That little boy felt so lost. There are parts of ourselves we need to reclaim. A quiet thought comes to mind, "What you seek is reconciliation with yourself." I call out to that small, frightened child-self and reassure him, "Hey, it's okay. You don't have to Try Harder or be The Strong One anymore. I'm here now", hoping nobody can hear me talking to myself. Paper Plate Man comes to mind, his smile, "Be here, be happy". I imagine that child-self standing taller on the beach, thrusting his shoulders back, looking out at the restless Solent tide, as if he knows somewhere inside his new soul that one day he won't need to retreat into his head so much, that he will return home to a map to turn a red dot blue, like the scabbing of a wound in the process of healing itself.

Back home, in the quiet, there is just the hum of the boiler which has somehow self-healed without mechanical intervention and is generating power again. I pick up the blue pen and colour the dot on the map, wondering if the island of childhood and mainland of adulthood have been re-joined and if the Bleep-Bleeping will now stop.

Three dots run. It was all going so well.

HOPE VALLEY

Where we are shapes who we become

Tent, stove, two sleeping bags, a plastic snow shovel and lots of soup. It is all packed in the car and the key is in the ignition when the email arrives: "Event cancelled" in the subject line in capital red letters. Attached to the email are photographs from Dartmoor of five foot high snow drifts at the entrance to the field where Race HQ should be situated. Okay, abandon Plan A.

Instead of camping in sub-zero temperatures and navigating Dartmoor the next day, Plan B means driving to the nearby Burton Dassett hills, one of Warwickshire's highest points, popular with kite fliers. What they don't have in Dartmoor's expanse is made up for in sharp elevations, deep creases in the landscape caused by quarrying ironstone in the late nineteenth century. They are awkward and hostile to run over when cloaked in ice but provide a 360 degree view of Warwickshire cascading into Oxfordshire. It is a place where you can see where you are. Rewind the clock 190 million years and the scene would have been a subtropical sea, teeming with sea urchins, squid-like belemnites and clams. Today, under a sun which hangs like a massive snow ball frozen in time against an ice-blue sky, there is just the metal shells of lorries and cars wiggling down the M40 motorway. This area used to lay nearer the equator. The Jurassic sea would have occasionally turned the colour of oxtail soup when storms washed iron-rich soil from nearby coastal forests, its legacy still found here as oyster, scallop and brachiopod fossils.

I run and clamber around Burton Dassett until the watch battery dies and despite wearing two pairs of gloves, my hands become too numb to grip and climb ice-skinned slopes. Seventeen miles of near-constant ascent and descent provides unexpected but much-needed training, but is not enough to count as a marathon. I watch the horizon suck the sun down, casting a red-fingered spotlight upon where I stand, as if blood puddles at my feet. To my right stands an isolated wooden gate with no fence either side of it, leading nowhere. Or everywhere.

I consider Plan C. Factoring in budget limits, winter weather, part-time work, childcare and recovery from the day-long Burton Dassett run means Plan C finally becomes Plan P, which is how I came to run in the Peak District on a Monday morning.

About 8,000 years ago, Hope Valley within which Ladybower reservoir rests, was a woodland of silver birch and oak, its ancient remains still visible in the cloughs. In the 1940s the valley was deliberately flooded, including the villages of Derwent and Ashopton, to supply millions of people with clean water. The valley, pock-marked with old lead mines, runs from east to west, twisting between the gritstone moors of the Dark Peak and the deep-cut dales and limestone crags of the White Peak. I have a 1957 cloth map of the area which smells of libraries, its original price eight shillings. The map shows the area around Ladybower reservoir as a broad smudge of toffee-brown, indicative of barren moorland. Twelve miles to the west is Kinder Scout, the highest peak in the Peak District at 2087 feet above sea level, celebrated for the mass trespass events in 1932 when ramblers clashed with gamekeepers demanding rights of access. Depending on which reports you believe, several hundred ramblers made their way to the plateau of

Kinder Scout. The protests led to short jail sentences for the trespass leaders, but arguably made way for the National Parks legislation in 1949, including the creation of the Penine Way and other long-distance footpaths. From this also came what we now recognise as the Countryside Code which outlines appropriate conduct for those rambling. It is easy to take our inheritance for granted, the freedom to walk, roam, run, climb, and enjoy vast expanses of our island, forgetting that it was rebellion and disruption that made these freedoms possible.

Parking by the Old Fisheries Centre, the skin of Ladybower gleams like aluminium. Last nights fall of snow has almost vanished from the hills. In the centre of the reservoir rests a boat, in the boat squats a man, fishing rod raised, his silhouette reflected onto the water.

Valleys tend, in geographic terms, to either be U-shaped or V-shaped, geologic depressions greater in length than width. They come in diverse forms: dells; glens; straths; coves; cloughs; hollows; steepheads. There is something ominous about valleys. They cut deep.

Two grey herons cross in the sky-path above as I begin running, their wings hooked over like the letter m, gliding toward the ground as if on invisible threads. Pushing through a metal gate with the latch missing, I move away from the noise of Snake Road and feel like I am entering the landscape, as if before I was somehow separate from it. My dad sometimes drove this way using the Snake Pass when I was a child and our family made the six-hour trip from Hampshire to visit my grandparents in Glossop on the edge of the Peak District. We usually stopped halfway at Woodstock where as children we would thrust our hands and feet into the wooden stocks and laugh at the idea of having rotten fruit thrown at us, like the criminals before us. The gate squeaks shut. I glance over my shoulder and notice the seven arches of the bridge I have run across reflecting in the water OOOOOOO like a chain of completed life-cycles.

Continuing into the hush of the woods, it still feels foreign to make choices without anyone else's permission, to be uncoupled from long-held loyalties where layers of expectation and assumption controlled the parameters about what was and wasn't allowed. To be writing my own rules, inking my own map.

Fearfall Woods doesn't exist on my eight shilling cloth map version of this place but it does in reality. Its steep-sloping woodland, layered with fallen pine needles obscuring pot holes, causes me to lose traction and I plunge, landing prostrate like an arrow, head and arms bowing in worship toward the reservoir. Both gloves rip, mud shovelling up my coat sleeves and clogging my beard. I have fallen in the first mile because I was paying more attention to my thoughts than my feet. Returning to the car, I curse beneath my breath "you're so bloody stupid, STUPID!" I clean myself up, sigh and start again. The fisherman remains motionless in the boat upon the water-skin as if the entire valley revolves around him.

Sanity is more than being "in your right mind". In fact, the origins of our word "sanity" weren't about being in your mind at all. The word comes from the Latin *sanare* meaning "to heal and be healthy", and *sanus* meaning "soundness", as in safe ground, hence sanctuary or safe place. Sanity means to be connected to the earth. Sanity can also be traced to an Old Norse word *helge* meaning "sacred, holy or wholeness". This dislocation between the mind and body runs deep in our psyche. It was only in the Enlightenment that its meaning got frog-marched upstairs to the rational mind, as far from the ground as it could get. Five minutes of watching the evening news or scrolling on social media confirms that collectively we are not in our right minds. Our immediacy of contact with the earth has evaporated and the devastating impact on human and planetary health is evident. In fact, the origin of "human" is *humus*, meaning "of the earth". In the Greek myth, Heracles understands that our power comes from contact with the ground and defeats the desert-dwelling wrestler Antaeus by lifting him off the earth. We are neither ghosts nor gods. We are not just a head floating in the atmosphere full of tremendous thoughts. We are earthbound creatures. We have idioms for this connection with the ground too: *Thinking on your feet; standing your ground; digging your heels in; staying on your toes.* We are an extension of the thing we crawl, stand, lay and run upon. We should let our feet do the thinking more often.

In coaching, I often ask not only "Who helps you?" and "What helps you?" but also "Where helps you?" Safe places might include mental states we create, such as a positive memory we replay that triggers feelings of appreciation, or physical things we do, hold, taste or smell. But we also need physical safe places, "geographies of hope", to borrow Wallace Stegner's resonant phrase. By naming them we notice them, by noticing them we practise them, and by practising them they become part of our fabric of recovery. We can draw strength from the ordinary places we inhabit: the weighted feel of the duvet; the quiet spot at the bottom of the garden; a treasured view from a window; a familiar bench in the park; the faithful pathway through a wood; a walk along a shoreline; a favourite seat on the bus or in a particular café. The familiarity of a place can soothe, becoming a sanctuary for both body and mind. A sense of temporary arrival, contact with here-and-now. There is no "cut along the dotted line" to scissor ourselves apart from the environments within which we breathe, speak and think. Where we are shapes who we become.

I pass the aqueduct and reach Fairholmes where Derwent Dam separates Ladybower and Derwent reservoirs. A village used to breathe near here, a village emptied to make way for the reservoirs. Bodies in Derwent church graveyard were moved to nearby Bamford and the remains of Derwent village church, post office and 17th century Derwent Hall can sometimes be seen in the summer protruding from the mud-bed like drowning arms, locked in a state of distress. Further on, where two tracks diverge, there are strange brick-humps erupting between trees: knee-high stone-stacked walls covered in lichen. For around a decade nearly a thousand people lived here in the "Navvy Village" of

Birchenlee, a pop-up village built by Derwent Valley Water Board for the workers on the valley dam and their families, plus shop keepers, a school teacher, a missioner, doctor and a policeman. It became known as "Tin Town" due to its corrugated iron roofs. The lichen-cloaked walls reveal floor plans of now extinct homes and shops. I stop where the Derwent Canteen once stood. The People's Refreshment House Association ran a canteen to try and control alcohol consumption by the workforce and it proved so popular the canteen was extended twice. I sit on its wall, the solid cold pressing into my buttocks and pour a mug of hot squash, listening to the sound of the pour. A trickle becomes a torrent, steam searching for shape.

What is buried here? I wonder. *What conversations happened? What stories have these trees overheard? What has this ground felt, suffered and sustained?* I imagine the present moment as a dot on a continuum, between the Beginning of Time and the End of Everything (it's quite a long line to try and imagine). *What is still to come? How far back along the continuum would I have to go to consider the first person who ever trod on this precise patch of earth? How far into the future will this place survive? How will it change because of the climate crisis?* I have no idea where the tiny dot called "now" sits between the two polarities of time. I feel heat in my hands from the mug and chill in my legs from the wall.

Peeling off my ripped glove, I gather a handful of common alder, oak and birch leaves. I feel a wave of sadness of how temporary all this is, how easily life crumbles between fingers. Erling Kagge, the polar explorer, speaks of the stars being a "silent, ever-present witness" which, when we contemplate them, can adjust our perspective so we take the long view, rather than surrendering to our usual myopia of "how am I doing today?". I find fallen leaves have a similar effect, but are closer than stars. Star-death is a slow drama, whereas leaves are quicker at making way for more life. I can crumble them between finger and thumb, observe their decay. I finish the hot squash, shaking drops from the mug onto the fallen leaves leaving a temporary constellation of wet dots.

Running through pine-woodland, the forest floor is knotted with knuckled roots. I need to pay attention if I don't want to plummet face-first again. There is a delicate stillness but I am struck more by absence, than presence; an absence of wildlife I hoped to see: golden plover, curlew, redstarts. What is present is litter in the most extraordinary places: two white supermarket-branded plastic bags, stuffed with beer cans, plastic bottle lids, maroon-coffee cups with the letters COST-pressed against the inside of the bag like a suppressed warning. The bags are tied with a lovely bow, as if two humans sat here and held a conversation about how important it is to gather up all your litter and tie it neatly in a disposable bag for someone else to collect from the edge of the reservoir. *How hard is it to join the dots between what we do and the impact on where we are? When we throw things away, where is 'away' specifically?* I run with the bags for several miles until I find a place where forestry commission vehicles park and leave them there. Sometimes life feels full of small futile acts of decency born from an inability to surrender final hope.

I arrive at the castled towers of Howden dam which appear like a pair of rooks on a chessboard, LLI_____LLI, crowns silhouetted against sky, and water streaks between the towers, over the spillway. At the apex of the three reservoirs, Ladybower, Derwent and Howden, is Slippery Stones. I expect to find large stones to traverse but there is only an old packhorse bridge, moved from the now long-gone Derwent village. A dilemma: I can either continue down the other side of the three reservoirs or wander out onto Howden Moor. I feel as if a hidden elastic connection between my body and the worn path is about to be broken. Stooping to a stream tumbling off the moor, I scoop up water in both hands, splash my face to wash away dirt, sweat and thought, and run onto the open moor. The sweet-song of a single blackbird cheers me in ways I cannot fathom as I run past a line of silver birch trees, their trunks flaking like old wallpaper, each unveiling a new, vibrant skin beneath. As I enter the moorscape of rich, dirty earth-tones, I realise I have gone off the map, or at least the version that is folded in my backpack.

During those blurred, liminal years where days bled into night and my nights swam with dark thoughts and enigmatic dreams, the silver St. Christopher pendant given at my birth but mislaid and forgotten for more than 20 years showed up. It was resting in an oblong brown box like a body in a coffin. The iconic image of the Saint was at the centre of the pendant, half bent like a crooked tree, up to his knees in a fast-flowing stream. He carried the burden of the Christ-child on his shoulders, the weight of a god who has not yet mastered walking on water. I held the pendant in my palm. For a few days I considered polishing the pendant and wearing it again. It was given with loving intentions in the earliest days of my life when my neural map was being configured. But to me it resembled the "good child" I had always tried to be. I'd been christened, confirmed and baptised into the church and given 40-plus years to serving it. The problem with ideology - whether religious, political or economic - is you don't ever believe you are wrong. Ideology offers a false promise that the world is "Absolutely Like This". If love is blind, then ideology is deaf. I didn't want to be burdened anymore by the narrow-minded version of religion I had subscribed to since birth, rampant with homophobia and demeaning women who dared to lead. I took the delicate silver chain between my index finger and thumb and gripped the pendant itself, not much bigger than a five pence piece, in the other fist. I wrenched the chain, once, twice, three times, until it laid on the oak dining table looking like a miniature person had walked free of shackles. A tiny act, of both anger and liberation.

William Bridges, in his Transitions theory, talks about the five "D's" which are intrinsic aspects of a transition, often experienced in "the nowhere zone" between endings and beginnings. He mentions *Disengagement*, when we become separate from our familiar contexts, roles and routines. There is *Dismantling*, as we unpack our previous life, often without any sense of what happens next. Transitions break up our old sense of self, as we *Disidentify* from who we thought we were and what we believed, a vulnerable experience threatening our sense of existence. But it was the *Disenchantment* which threw me, the breaking of the old spell. The realisation that the religious ideals in my head were not the Truth. The dawning sense I had somehow been tricked by those around me. And as the illusions evaporated, *Disorientation* took over big time.

I plunged deeper into my present to clear out the past, locating mementos, certificates and souvenirs that connected me to people, places and perspectives whose burden I no longer wanted on my shoulders. The months that followed included tearing up dozens of boxes of photos so faces and places bore ripped edges like white lightning; deleting three social media accounts; emptying my entire wardrobe and choosing garment by garment whether it stayed or went; ripping each page of more than 25 years of hand-written journals into strips, each contained within black leather skins. When stacked one upon the other the journals rose to a height of nearly a metre, like a mini-tower of Babel. The page-ripping took six hours, an old script in my brain feeling betrayed, each rip sounding like striking a match against the box. Shredding each page, fingers pinching then parting in opposite directions, was like removing the litter so my mind could breathe, hear, heal. The next day my arms felt two inches longer. I smashed photograph frames. Took scissors to two large paintings given as a gift. Binned computer memory sticks with a decade of work and research projects on them. Discarded every religious book on my shelves. Tore up my university dissertation, its title in gold lettering "Light at the End of the Tunnel" glinting under the lounge lightbulb before its cliché was extinguished forever.

One morning I awoke and before opening the curtains the first act of the day, yielding to a gut impulse, was to remove every branded loyalty card from my wallet until a single supermarket card remained (because I had to shop somewhere). Loyalty became singular. A slim-fast diet for the wallet. I scissor-cut the shirt of the football team I had supported since childhood, throwing out the red and white striped woolly hats, scarves, mugs, match day programmes. A friend called my change in loyalties "fickle". I called it choice. I unplugged from daily news, unsubscribed from every newsletter and stopped watching television for four years. Others worried I was isolating myself but I could feel the gift of headspace and a connection to myself I had never previously known. For months, self-care wasn't treating myself to a raspberry muffin, it was separating, snapping, smashing, scissoring, tearing, twisting, terminating, binning, removing, erasing, crushing, liberating, untying, unwiring. Unwiring neurons I wish had never met. *You put together two things that have not been put together before and the world is changed.* I was detaching from the past in order to see it more clearly and my neurons went hunting for a new future.

Howden Moor acts like a Chinese-box, a canvas opening further out from within itself. With each soft foot-thud, the discursive mind eases back. Thinking reclines to the background and a silent undertone comes to the fore. At times like this something entirely unaccountable can arise. An insight. A previously unseen connection between two things. Something out there in the world and something in here combine, dot joins dot, neurons meet for the first time and settle down together. Snip-snip, the blades of thought and environment interact and the fabric of experience is reshaped. A smile begins, hope rekindles, wonder returns. You never know what your next thought will be.

With fifteen miles run I notice distance between thoughts. The clinging thoughts of a small-self ebb away as if over a spillway. Thoughts flicker, fade and fall, giving up the effort of being substantial. Shoulders relax, body lowers like a return to earth. Breath deepens, from throat to chest to gut until finally all the weight drops to the feet, a descent requiring time, space and place.

I scan the moorland, hoping to see a goshawk, then stare into damp woodland where, although unlikely, I might spot a woodcock. I stop and listen for the distinctive drum-beat drilling of a male woodpecker.

But all I hear is breath, feet, the sloosh-sloosh of my water bottle. In wintertime there are reportedly white mountain hares on the moor but today the landscape is a spectrum of sweet browns. As the thin pebbled moor path comes to an end I continue running unbound across the moor. Somewhere beneath Crow Stones Edge, I stop again and stare at the horizon until my feet feel the pull to return if I am to safely complete the run before nightfall.

Stepping through pine debris and sawdust I meet the reservoir edge and am confronted by rocks twice my height through which I cannot squeeze. I heave myself up and over the rock and weave through an area of newly planted saplings until I reunite with a familiar track. As the track twists, bends and descends, my pace quickens. A sign on a hairpin bend warns cyclists against going over the edge. I reach the bend slightly out of control, sunlight rips through birch branches, blinding me, causing me to run directly between a man and woman who have stopped in the centre of the track to share a packet of biscuits. Their snacks shatter across the path, the lady yelps and the man flings his arms up as if in surrender. I spin and run backwards down the hill waving at them in silent apology.

Returning to the Old Fisheries with 23 miles run, I lean against the passenger door of the car and swig lukewarm black coffee. The skin of the reservoir blushes pink beneath the bright white capital **D** of the moon, a bright thumbprint upon the sky. Vapour trails stretch like tyre marks into infinity. With dusk descending, clusters of pine trees lose individual distinction and everything blends to singularity. But the run is not yet done. I made a promise to myself: *however long the process takes, just keep going*. I head out again, running through the dusk-dark Fearfall Woods once more, trusting my feet to find the way and hoping not to fall.

SPRING

"I have gone ahead despite the pounding in the heart
that says turn back"

—Erica Jong

At Warwick service station off the M40 motorway, a short dash from Burton Dasset hills, I sit in the corner of the café at a table with space for six. The window stretches from floor to ceiling to maximise the light. Hand-written signs on A4 paper adorn the windows: PLEASE RETURN YOUR DIRTY ITEMS TO THE TROLLEY except the sign above my head has the bottom half torn off: PLEASE RETURN YOUR DIRT... Outside, a lady in hiking boots with large tongues and loose laces tends a small box hedge, scratching the ground with a trowel, permanently bent over like a hinge as if all history rides upon her shoulders.

Before me rests a stack of loose paper printouts, thin cardboard folders and books. I am here to absorb the names and stories of map-makers from the past whose cartographical legacy spills across the table: Anaximander, Bordone, Ptolemy, Vespucci, Martellas, Ribeiro, Barbari. I am late to the map-loving craze. To me maps were inherited fixed truths of how things are. You obeyed maps, their two-dimensional authority telling you the lie of the landscape. But as I turn pages, flip sheets, surrender myself to the process of unfolding and decreasing, I realise the past is not as honest as we are told. Whomever forms the map forms the mind.

The lady by the box hedge outside stretches her arms in the air, saluting the sun.

Over thousands of years maps have been drawn in sand, soil, charcoal, on fig tree fibres, clay and stone. Sea-faring mariner's used sheepskin vellum to preserve maps from deterioration caused by salt water. Native Americans used bison hide and the Algonquin people used kernels of corn to interpret their landscapes. One of my favourites are the World War Two pilots who had escape maps printed onto silk scarves which they scrunched into bomber jacket pockets.

Maps present a reality frozen in time, so it is easy to forget how much is constantly on the move, like tree sap, pollen, roots, fungi, water vapour. Today we are used to screen-maps we pinch, swipe, scroll and zoom in and out from, to get the perspective we want. I once met a man out walking on Kinder Scout in the Peak District who was lost on the Penine Way. "That line of hills" he said to me, pointing down toward a craggy valley, "according to my phone, they shouldn't be there." Maps are not only about how we see the world, but how we want to see it.

I had no idea there were so many different ways of seeing the same thing. Sometimes a map is about an idea rather than reality. A woodcut map by Heinrich Bünting in 1581 shows the world arranged as a clover leaf, with Africa at the bottom and Europe and Asia above it. At the centre is the city of Jerusalem, the three-leaf clover representing the Christian Trinity. I look through disorienting maps where East is at the top and North is thrust to the side, and Saint-Sever Beatus maps where the world is depicted as a circle divided internally by a T-shape, with Asia at the top and Britain plopped as a sausage-shape in the margins. Maps are not just for telling you where you are, they show what is known or unknown - terra incognita; they explain what has been explored or exploited, and to whom a place belongs. Maps illuminate natural boundaries and thresholds, be they coastlines, rivers or mountain ranges. They might focus on interior divisions, political divides or geologic structures. Maps help to discern routes, track patterns, conceal secrets or reveal discoveries.

Maps for survival, protection, navigation, declaration, connection, exploitation, revelation, legacy. Maps to limit possibilities and maps to expand them.

The oldest surviving model globe made from two different ostrich eggs at the start of the 16th century by Martin Behaim depicts what the New World looked like and is from where we get the phrase "Hic sunt dracones": "Here be dragons".

Maps have edges we are warned away from.

WICKEN FEN

Beginning again is available

The car radio is on. "Storm Freya will be arriving this afternoon bringing gales of up to 80mph." I spin the volume dial to the right. "Forecasters have issued weather warnings with the storm set to last until tomorrow morning. Heavy rain will cause delays for motorists." The warning is followed by music, "In Paradisium" from Fauré's Requiem. The omens are not good.

A week ago we experienced the highest February temperature on record. I watched a man walk down the village high street, a white t-shirt hanging from the waistband of his shorts, his sandals slapping a sun-lit pavement as he licked an ice-cream from the bottom of the cone to the top. Today, early Spring reveals its shadow-side, manifesting winter in a wink. Clouds squat on the A14 road towards Cambridge, giant wind turbines rotating their long arms in frantic unison to an invisible deity. Tourniquets of white plastic sheeting stream from oak trees. Windscreen wipers rub away dots and dashes of rain, a message in morse code: ... - --- .--.. The message is wiped away. It reappears. Wiped away. Reappears. Driving over Earith Bridge, it is not wildness one sees, but vacuity, as if the landscape has surrendered to the sheer weight of sky. In this horizontal plain, place names flow with watery associations: Waterbeach, Landbeach, Horningsea, The Washes.

Arriving at Wicken Fen National Nature Reserve, the car park is almost empty. This is the oldest nature reserve in the country, popular with Victorian naturalists. Charles Darwin apparently collected beetles from here as part of his research 200 years ago. A man, trapped in a winter coat, wrestles with an inverted umbrella, head down as he tries to bring it under control like a misbehaving pet. I lay an Ordnance Survey map across the steering wheel. The waterways, thought to be of Roman origin, look like forked lightning, cracking across the surface. I have no idea how to penetrate this place. The Cambridgeshire Fens are hardly the outback but preparation matters. I drop a first aid kit and aluminium foil blanket into a rucksack. Then the essentials go in: a family-sized pork pie, two rounds of ham sandwiches and five snack bars.

A marooned rowing boat outside the visitor centre marks my imaginary start line. I begin running, skirting St. Edmund's Fen, before running alongside Monk's Lode then turn right towards Priory Bridge. Ecclesiastic names offer no sanctuary from the weather. The wind sounds like a trombone, constantly exhaling, stuck on a single note, as if in the act of giving birth. Lines of sedge reeds bow low. Fields the colour of cocoa lay dormant. Half a dozen Highland cattle, ginger fringes flopping between horns, occupy all four corners of a field as if having time out from each other. The landscape is a graveyard for farm machinery, tractor wheels bandaged in reeds, weeds, briars, brambles, knotted by nettles. How did they end up here with all their best days behind them? I turn from Adventurer's Fen, continuing along Burwell Lode, a long groove of water where two hooded men pass in the opposite direction, each holding a fishing rod erect like a car aerial, as if fishing in the sky for answers.

The wind hammers me into submission as I run, chin chastened to chest, attention lifted only by the sight of a kestrel five metres ahead. With its wings flapping in wild excitement it hovers in aerial liminality, before swooping, twisting, flashing its chestnut back, then rising and hovering again. Both of us are mesmerised, me by the bird, and the bird by what it spies on the ground. Its body remains motionless in the fierce wind, an axle around which everything else in the universe turns, before it glides with the ease of exhalation, steering itself down, round and away. I run backwards, admiring the kestrel as we part ways.

At Burwell village I drop the backpack against the wall of The Anchor pub and lean against the wall for refuge from the wind. My chest feels tight and legs heavy, as if I have run 20 miles not four. I am in search of a windmill. The map writhes in my hands, tugging to escape, so it's impossible to trace a route. The intention is to run along Devil's Dyke, a seven mile scar across the map between the villages of Reach and Woodditton, crossing three roman roads and dissecting two different ecosystems: a chalk escarpment on one side and a peat fenland on the other. The dyke is an ancient defensive earthwork structure probably built by East Anglian Saxons, around the 6th or 7th century, a barrier against the Britons and now designated as a Site of Special Scientific Interest (SSSI). In some places it rises more than nine metres from ditch to ridge, hedgerows on either side acting as wildlife corridors which today become a shield.

Everything in Burwell is closed except The Elk café from which spills the aroma of coffee and human conversation. A tempting haven. Turning a corner I run smack into a tree and become entangled in its branches. Sugar-pink blossom explodes from its twisted fingertips, a tree fecund with joy, a striking contrast to both the weather and place. I wriggle in an attempt to duck beneath its branches which scratch my face, until I am surrounded by a skirt of flowers, intoxicated by fragrance. I stop fighting with the tree and instead inhale its blossom scent and stroke its petals. A man in a Barbour jacket stands and frowns as if to say, "how dare you smile on a day like this?"

I need to get out of Burwell. I run past the old railway station, towards Devil's Dyke, turning from the road and feel, just briefly, the hedgerow softening the persistent pinch of wind. A yellowhammer appears like a flying banana, flying out from a heap of brambles chasing a chaffinch. Then they are gone, snatched by the wind. Clambering up onto the dyke-ridge, clawing at rocks, I get a long view across the fen.

It is a bereft, grieving landscape, as if whatever was here has gone forever. Sliding down a steep chalky bank, I step across a disused railway line, before heaving up the other side, past stunted rowan and hawthorn bushes, fruitless and full of thorn. A discarded woollen hat has been placed over the top of a stile like an executioner's balaclava. Another omen.

At the entrance to Reach village is a monument near to where the dyke begins or ends, depending on your direction of travel. A local story says the Devil came here uninvited to a wedding but was chased away by the guests, the deep ditch created by the drag of his tail as he stormed off. The monument shows an embossed child sitting upon a horse on a merry go round, child clinging to the pole, petrified, the horse with a look of insanity, its teeth bared. No wonder the Devil ran away. The map shows a route around the back of the village, along Barston Drove, towards Swaffham Prior. Everything feels unfamiliar: the lodes, sedge reeds, the dyke, the inertia of space, the windmill I am searching for. Running here is like stroking the face of a stranger in the dark, trying to decipher from its features its personality and temperament. This place seems fought over, wounded, abandoned. Can there be anything to love here, a place so full of absence? Continuing along the B1102 towards Swaffham Bulbeck my pace slows. I clutch my chest. The passing cars are all black or silver, as if yanked back in time. I cross Gutter Bridge Ditch. The place name says it all.

Passing through the village of Lode, I arrive at Anglesey Abbey, a Jacobean house and gardens owned by the National Trust. A Giant Redwood tree stands at the entrance like a three-pronged devil's fork, fractured by being struck by lightning twice, twelve years apart at the end of the last century. Entering the Abbey foyer I notice an immediate surge in temperature. My face tingles. Breath shortens. "I... hello, I need...help" I say. A lady with a blurred face stares at me as I stoop, squat, then crawl along the tiled floor into the busy café before laying prostrate. I am a heap of wet fluorescence surrounded by an army of metal chair legs. A staff member, James, crouches over me to check if I am okay and offers ginger cake. "It's Pauline's cake" he says, "she makes some each time she comes in". A cup of sweet milky tea is placed on a table which I can neither reach nor have the strength to lift. Whitman asked "What do you stand for?" but I can't stand for anything right now, not even Pauline's ginger cake, although if I could I would take her cake ahead of world peace. When the shivering begins it feels like something unravelling from deep inside. I can't go on like this. "Did you know ginger...." I begin to say but James looks puzzled as he hands me the cake. "Did you...ginge...ginger... anti-inflamm prop-tees?" I mumble before wedging the cake into my mouth in one go. For the next hour James checks my pulse and stares into my eyes to see if anybody is home. "Does this happen often?" he asks. I recall lying on my back in a white marquee after my first marathon in London, attached to a saline drip; I recall rushing behind a parked ambulance after the Guernsey marathon to vomit on a bed of roses; I recall slumping unconscious on my toilet at home after a 22 mile run, contributing to a minor heart arrest and an ambulance ride to hospital. I look at James - although he seems to have an identical twin next to him - both of him have such innocent faces. "No, James" I lie, "it's never been like *this* before". He holds up his fingers for me to count. I think there are eight but he might just be giving me a double-V sign. James helps me onto a chair. "We are closing now, just so you know" he says.

Pulling the map from the saturated backpack, with a pale finger I trace a route back to Wicken Fen where the car awaits. The watch indicates only 11.9 miles run, not even halfway. The most direct route back is nine miles along the Droveway, then alongside the River Cam. My phone vibrates. It's my partner, Jess, checking how I am. "I'll be okay in a bit" I reassure her, cake crumbs tumbling across the map. "If you run back to Wicken Fen" she says, "in these conditions", I watch rain lashing the café window ... - — .—.. "and let's say three miles in you collapse again, who's going to help you?" I consider the possibility of James not hearing me whistling from so far away. I consider the absence of Pauline's ginger cake. Instead, as the Abbey staff get ready to shut the premises, I take Jess' advice and phone a taxi company. For £30.20 I am back at my car within an hour, shivering and stinking of the cigarette that remained hooked on the lip of the taxi driver as he sped down potholed lanes, swerving to avoid stray chickens and other vehicles. I climb into my own driving seat. Rain scrapes the windscreen as the car rocks in the wind, as if attempting to shake it from slumber. A mug lodged between my knees steams the windscreen until I can no longer see out and nobody can see in.

At the Youth Hostel Association in Cambridge I drag my feverish body plus suitcase up three flights of stairs, before collapsing exhausted, still in sodden running kit, onto an unmade bed and remain there until the early hours of the morning when the hostel fire alarm screams into life. The snoring of six men stops in unison as a young man leaps from his top bunk, slaps on the dormitory light, illuminating every contour of his naked body. He jumps up several times to punch the smoke alarm on the ceiling which then crashes to the floor, his penis slapping the inside of his thigh, nodding in delight with each jump. The room light goes out. The trauma from the day has followed me here. There is no ginger cake. I fail to sleep. When I get home the next day, I go to bed and sleep for three days until the fever passes.

A few weeks later, back in Stratford-upon-Avon, hurrying down Henley Street near the birthplace of William Shakespeare, a crowd of tourists blocks the path. A man dressed in brown, as though he has been rolling through mud, sits on a tall stool. His eyes are closed as he plays a slim electric double bass. Music unfurls like the semi-quavers of his hair, sounding rich and serene. He, or it, or this ineffable thing that is happening, mesmerises me. I stop. It is like penetrating an invisible threshold. "Your music" I say to him between songs, "seems to come from a different place, from something deep inside you". His eyes moisten, then he tells me a story. "I once lost everything" he says, gripping the neck of his bass. "My home, my wife, my work. All I was left with was music. To be honest, I didn't know how to start again." The tourists take photos around us but don't seem to be listening. "Let me tell you what happened" he says. "I went to a charity shop and bought this jacket for a couple of quid" and he flaps the breast of the jacket. "When I got back to my mate's flat I checked the left pocket and there was a £50 note in it." As I laugh, he interrupts, "no, hang on...because then I checked the right pocket and there was another £50 note in there too." His eyes are wide and piercing. "What did you do?" I ask. "I took it back to the shop to see if they could trace the donors, which they did. But the donors said that perhaps it was meant to be, that I could keep the money." He levers the double bass back and forth, like a metronome. "So when I stand here and play," he looks at the crowd waiting behind me, "I remember that I am provided for. I remember I am sustained, somehow. Every note of my music is a gesture of gratitude in return for the chance to begin again".

Starting and Beginning are not the same thing. This is important to know in the transitions we make, and the attitude we bring to the day. Our word "start" comes from a Dutch word *storten* meaning "to push" and a German word *stürzen* meaning "to fling" or "fall headlong into". There is a sense of impulse, a force of effort. Sure, sometimes we need to start stuff, but there can be something quite angry, or grabbing about the push, the chase, the relentless treadmill of productivity. "Beginnings" are different. They have a different texture to them. Think about beginnings in your own life - a relationship, vocation, adventure. Did they just happen or was there a gradual process? What were the tiny easy-to-miss moments that were part of the beginning? Our word "beginning" has obscure origins (which is interesting) and probably means "to open up". How did you "open up" to the new thing, person, place, opportunity? I often try to "start" things, sensing the finitude of time on earth and my Achiever Self wanting to get stuff done. There's a bit of ego in my Starting Stuff, an impatience with the process. But every transition I have ever made has required time, trust, help, enquiry, risk taking, some failing, and a deeper level of listening.

Beginnings are always available but not entirely in our control. Walking through a local village one morning wondering how on earth I could start a business without any cash and debts of £16,000 from solicitor fees and buying a second hand car, a man I recognised but didn't know well waited for me at the Saxon bridge with his dog. At a time when it was hard to talk to anyone because of the shame of divorce and unemployment, I was surprised when he looked me in the eye, smiled and said "hello". As we walked the local meadow together, he let me talk. Returning to the bridge half an hour later, he looked me in the eye again. "I'm going to make an offer" he said, "work out what you need to set up your business, I will lend you the money, interest-free. No deadlines for repayment." My knees went to jelly, the traffic crossing icon turned green, and that was sorted. Around this time I dreamed about a lady I knew who invited me into her office and asked for help. The next day I risked emailing her to ask what help she needed (not mentioning the dream as that would be weird). Within an hour she replied offering me two hours work a week. It was a beginning. A few months later through her connections I had three days work a week, enough to rent a flat and slowly pay off the debt. My business started the same day as moving in. "Sorry about the Aston Villa colours in the bedrooms" the landlord said, "I'll get them painted" and within 24 hours the flat stank of whitewashed walls. That same week, in a conference meeting room six floors up, overlooking Coventry, a lady whom I had never met sat directly opposite me and began speaking to the group. After several minutes, in the middle of a sentence, she stopped abruptly and stared at me. "You need to know that you will find your way" she said, holding my eye contact for a few seconds, before continuing to speak to the rest of the group. I felt held by something beyond myself (and her words are still with me today, six years on). None of this help was deserved, expected or contrived, but the weaving of the recovery process operates quietly in the background. Survive. Return. Restore.

Occasionally, when coaching, I invite others to write the sentence "I have survived..." at the top of a blank page, and then to list for themselves all the failures, break-ups and bereavements which they have already come through. Gathering together their fractured life experiences under one heading of "survived" provides a shortcut to being in contact with their own resilience. Then new sentences: "From these experiences, I have learned... I have received... I have become..." This is the strange gift of grief, that it beckons us towards our capacity for strength, gratitude, learning, love.

Four weeks later, recovered in body and resolved in mind, I attempt a solo marathon across the fens, again. There are just 34 hours left before the end of March if I am going to complete a marathon within the month. Even if I cover one mile an hour, I reason, I can make it. Driving along the A14, James Morrison sings on the stereo "You're stronger than you know..." The landscape looks verdant, like licked lips ready to be kissed. The season has turned a corner, and I hope I have too. Arriving at Wicken Fen car park instead of there being up-turned umbrellas, families eat picnics and a pensioner reclines in a deckchair. In the interests of doing the run differently, I decide to run the route in reverse: find the river, follow it to Lode village, visit the Abbey to say thank you to James for the cake, and return via the Swaffhams. Easy.

Reeds line the fen edge like soldiers at attention. I cross Priory Bridge, passing two cyclists in hi-viz costumes trundling their bikes down the narrow metal ramp, then turn right, along Adventurer's Fen hoping to find the River Cam. Two herons swoop down using the lode like a landing strip, before rising again and curving left over the fields. A cormorant follows them, taking off from the watery runway, as sleek as calligraphy resurrected from the page. The contrast from the start of the month to now is palpable. The land has lift off. The sun strokes my forehead and everything across the land is lit yellow, like melting butter on toast. Thousands of miniature golden crowns of forsythia froth from hedgerows, cascading to earth; dandelions and daffodils parade their faces proudly; a clouded yellow butterfly with a tiny black dot on its wing waltzes at my waist. I spin as it circles me and I cannot help but laugh. It is a "welcome back", a reconciliation. Wicken Fen, all is forgiven.

By error, with five miles run, I arrive in Reach village where the child on the fairground horse looks as terrified as ever. Sitting on a bench beneath an oak on the village green the sun illuminates the map as it unfolds across my knees. The only sound is a man scraping turf from his drive with a spade. A magpie swoops, landing on a telephone wire, swinging its tail like a cricket bat. The stillness is something to love here. Tucking the wrinkled map away I breathe in the slowness. Next stop: The Abbey. But when I reach The Abbey and ask the staff about James and Pauline nobody knows who I mean. Either the staff rota has not worked in my favour or it was all hallucination.

Across Bottisham Fen I zig-zag across vacant land until reaching the River Cam. A man in a kayak eases his way with the current. With 22 miles run, Wicken Fen is lit by the peach-glow of a setting sun probing its way through walls of blackthorn blossom. In the fading light I run laps of Sedge Fen to reach the distance, sprinting as fast as I can along raised black boards above the marshland before it is too dark to see. Three muntjac deer leap across the path, startling me into a sudden stop, their distinctive white-pom hinds the last observable thing before they dive into the copse, all three together as if joined at the hip. They stop, turn, and stare again, before bounding off. I return to the car park, resting my hands on the car bonnet, as if practising resuscitation. The March marathon is complete with a day to spare. This red dot has proved a challenge, but hope is in the ascendancy. There is a word from the 16th century for this mood, now rarely used, *respair,* meaning "fresh hope and recovery from despair". The next dot involves running along a cliff edge.

JURASSIC COAST

Everything is always changing

A month on from battling Storm Freya on Wicken Fen, Storm Hannah arrives with 51mph winds across Dorset's Jurassic Coast. Between Freya and Hannah the least ominous sounding storm ever, Storm Gareth, rushed through. Naming helps with noticing. The alternating binary pattern of male and female names for storms was established in the 1970s by the National Hurricane Center in North America to raise public awareness that it is time to close windows, bring in the washing and reinforce fences. Storms tagged with names indicate it is not a time to go camping.

Driving the final two miles to the campsite are along lanes so narrow I hold my breath as I drive, fiddlehead ferns scrubbing the side of the car. Turning a sharp right into Eype Camping and Caravan site the car sings in first gear as it ascends the slope. I shouldn't be surprised as Eype means "steep place". I unravel the tent, spreading my body across the fabric to prevent slap-gusts of wind sprinting off with it. Where's Y-front Max when you need him? Despite nestling my stove next to the car tyre to shield it from the wind, the stove fails to stay lit for more than a few seconds, each flame suffocated to extinction by the last gasps of Storm Hannah.

I give up and walk down a hedge-lined lane to Eype beach, under the eye of the south coast's highest cliff, Golden Cap. Sun sinks into skin, sea shushes the ear, the tang-taste of salt fills the air. Research has shown that the sound of the sea changes our brain wave patterns, heightening relaxation, changing the way we think and what we feel. An invisible alchemy, brain waves tuning into sea waves, gamma to beta, beta to alpha, alpha to delta, where all streams of thought, sound and time converge. At the base of the steps to the beach the sea has snatched land so in the remaining inlet three rowing boats are upturned, looking abandoned in a hurry. Blue lias clay cliffs crumble, edges ripped away by the hydraulic action of sea and pebble abrasion.

The Jurassic Coast gets its name from the Jura mountains in the European Alps where limestone strata were first identified, the Jurassic period being the one sandwiched between the Triassic and Cretaceous epochs, stretches of time measured in millions of years. The cliffs here are part of a 95-mile World Heritage coastline recording 175 million years of changing earth history. The area is a rich hunting ground for fossils, especially ammonites. Fossils have played an important part in map-making, helping William Smith create the first geological map in 1815, the presence of ammonites helping to date rock sediment where fossils were found. Smith's scientific approach challenged widely held religious beliefs that the earth was only 6,000 years old. Fixed mental maps had to be reviewed in light of his discovery. Today, geological features can be identified by satellite imagery using different wavelengths of light so maps first crafted by digging deeper are now created by going higher.

Nothing sits still, neither the natural landscape, nor the human mind. Nature changes and to change is our nature. Internal and external are in ceaseless flux. Cliffs erode; land-plates riff and clash; mountains are thrust up and worn down; tree-rings map expansion year upon year; the stratification of sediment, rock, shells, sand, mud, all show up on a cliff face, along a sand dune or on the sea floor. Erosion, adaptation and expansion happen with humans too: skin cells regenerate around every 27 days; bones adapt to the loads they bear; axioms dance in the brain in search of forging new neural pathways; muscles strengthen and atrophy. Everything is always changing. We are life, and life is dynamic, fluctuating and unpredictable, like coastlines.

I visited coasts as often as I could during the months when I was without work or a secure base: Tenby, Brighton, Isle of Wight, Bournemouth, Skegness, Cromer, Aldeburgh, Porlock Weir. Sometimes with Jess but oftentimes alone just to walk and notice things. According to environmental psychologist Mathew White, who studied census data to find out the effect of sea air, those living within half a mile of the coast experience the greatest benefit. Sea air contains minerals which lower stress chemicals in the brain and improve alertness. Sea salt also preserves tryptamine, serotonin and melatonin levels in the brain, lessening the impact of low mood and helping improve quality of sleep. The long visual horizons which coasts offer decompress the brain and the soundtrack of tidal flow has rejuvenating benefits for the heart.

Approaching the tideline I think of my Uncle Andrew. During the years he had motor neurone disease, change meant he lost the ability to put on his own shoes and socks, couldn't hold a knife steady when eating casserole, or even nip to the newsagent for a paper like he used to do. Yet, although changed by the quiet onslaught of a terminal illness, he expanded with a patience and peacefulness I have rarely observed in another person. As strength eroded, serenity emerged.

A wave gapes, its upper lip rising, foaming at the mouth, before spitting onto the shingle, pausing, then gulping pebbles down its throat as it retreats into itself, like a yawn. The tide chews at the foundations. I clamber onto a rock jutting four feet up from the shingle, the same size as my tent but immovable by wind or time, then look along the coastline toward West Bay where a thousand tonnes of rock collapsed last month. A tidal surge with singular force rushes like a fist at the rock upon which I stand before exploding into ten thousand white particles, each disappearing out of sight, sucked into the sand with a sound like storm-breath.

Unzipping the tent at 5.45 a.m. the wind has quelled. In the frame of the open tent door a herring gull and crow tussle mid-air like yin-yang in flight. After cold porridge and cold coffee from a flask, I follow the usual marathon prep routine: lubricating between each toe and on both nipples, compression socks pulled knee-high, safety pins poised ready to anchor a race number in place. Organisers describe today's race as "brutal" which might just be marketing talk but it includes four loops of a 6.6 mile cliff-top route with staircase ascents and pot-holed descents of several hundred feet each.

Driving through West Bay to the race start there is a car boot sale in full swing, unless it is vehicle theft happening on a mass scale. Arriving in a field edged with event flags puttering in the wind, a man bangs thin plastic stakes into the ground. "You're a bit early mate!" he says, leaning through my passenger car window, waving his mallet at me. "Tell you what, you can be my guinea pig for the parking." I imagine a hammered guinea pig. "You don't have to pay for your parking, but don't tell anyone, yeah?" I swear to keep it a secret, forever.

"Aaaaallll right now, baby, you're aaaaallll right now" explodes over the sound system as 26 of us assemble in a gravel car park surrounded by empty cargo containers. We stand spaced apart ignoring one another. In a year this will be called "Social Distancing". Twenty-six runners. I wonder if everyone would be up for running just one mile each as a team relay. The race organiser calls us to the start line. This is so *not* the London marathon, also happening today, where 39,000 people from all over the world will run from the East end of London, past crowds with "Go Mummy!" banners and hoardings advertising carbohydrate-rich products, before finishing down The Mall. I miss the energy of the race crowd but the anonymity here is welcome. A man dressed like an Olympic skier stands with a walking pole in each hand, hi-tech sunglasses perched on his forehead like a dark screen over his thoughts. He explains, at volume, why he has masses of blue tape plastered around his right knee. "I ripped my quad muscle the other week doing a 103 mile run." The number 103 is said slowly to make sure we hear it. I haven't run a mile since Wicken Fen and instantly doubt whether I should even be in the car park. The organiser clears his throat. "Careful of the farmer at Hive Farm", he says, "I suspect he's removed all the event signage so, you know, look out!" widening his eyes and waving the mallet suggesting it could come in handy. "Okay, er...well, off you go then" he says, and 26 strangers stand and look at each other to see who wants to go first.

Darting up a slope in single file none of us are sure where we are going. The first runner wades through stinging nettles then hurdles a stretch of barbed wire leading onto a golf course. Three men wave their golf clubs in disbelief at the eruption of runners onto their perfectly manicured putting green. The route crosses several fields, passing caravan sites, before arriving at a small table by a gate loaded with chocolate waffles, peanuts and bananas, plus energy drinks in biodegradable cups. "Stuff your faces like it's a midnight feast!" urge the teenage girls marshalling the route.

The first major hill comes after two miles at Burton Bradstock where a sign pinned to a gate reads: "This is not a hill. It is just a bump on the route. The hills come later." Runners spread out ahead along the cliff edge, running over the sea thrift within two feet of the cliff edge which is cordoned off with red and white striped tape, panicking in the wind. There is nothing to stop anyone plunging over the edge if they slip.

A telegraph pole with a lifebuoy ring hung upon it marks the lap turning point. A volunteer sat beneath the lifebuoy gives instructions on how to literally go round the bend, circling his right arm above his head as if preparing to lasso a runner. The return route is mostly back along the cliff coastal path. Ahead, the Dorset landscape rises and falls, as if someone has shaken a tablecloth in the air and it is waiting to settle. Sudden descents of 200 feet sometimes come with stair rails, but mostly not, so I run with my arms out like wings, as if I am Kate

Winslet held by Leonardo DiCaprio on the front of the Titanic ship, wind rushing through my receding hairline.

The steep descent back into West Bay is full of pot holes, grassy lumps and onlookers huddled on the beach. A country lane leads us back toward the buttercup field, a scramble back through ferns and nettles, ready to begin the next loop. After two laps my knees feel the accumulation of lactate acid. After three laps - nearly 20 miles - my head is down and both feet feel hot. I try to "be mindful" by listening to gulls and watching an eight-person canoe battling out at sea but these sensory navigations don't last long before I am back inside my head, ruminating, calculating pace and distance and chasing a female runner with double blonde plaits ahead of me. There could be kestrels, curlews and ravens cruising past but I forget the vast expanse of possibility I am moving through, only aware of the cliff edge, my shuffling feet and the inevitable discomfort. Running along the cliff edge should feel invigorating but I can't pretend to feel something I don't. I wonder why the hell I'm here, doing this. I have no idea where to run next month or whether I want to continue this journey. Once again, the nagging noise in the brain speaks up, "what's the point?" Perhaps I should just try harder, fit in better, do as I'm told and mute the instinct which urges me to go beyond the familiar.

One night I disappeared into the ground. Pushing an empty wheelie bin back to where it belonged I stepped into nothing and fell down an uncovered manhole, falling so far down that only my head remained above ground level. It looked as if my head had become a football on the ground. At that particular point in my life there were people who would relish kicking this football-head of mine. I yelped. Lights appeared in neighbouring houses. People flung open their doors, "what's happened?" they shouted, "is everything alright? Anything we can do?" Disappearing had become an emergency.

Falling into old patterns of thought and replaying memories from yesterday is easy. Ping! And your awareness of the present has...gone! Here one moment but lost in thought the next. It can happen between the front door and the car. Between the reception and the office. Between one step and the next. Thoughts whisk us away from the body as if only our head exists on the earth and our full-body, multi-sensory contact with reality disappears until something gives us a nudge (or a kick) to return us to whatever process we are meant to be attending to, like putting the dustbin away, boiling the kettle, or running along a cliff edge. "When you are washing the dishes" said a Zen monk many years ago, "just wash the dishes."

As a young child my mother bought me a small plaque to hang on the wall by my bunk bed. The words were printed in calligraphic form, leaning forward like a promise: *Lord, help me remember that nothing is going to happen today that you and I can't handle together.* It was a sentiment that brought enormous comfort to me as a child, necessary scaffolding for a mind still under construction. Yet behind the sentiment lay a different, less helpful message which I introjected: "When you feel you can't cope, escape into your head". One thing experiencing liminality taught me was that I needed help training my mind to sit still and get some distance from the Old Beliefs that still paraded as Absolute Truths.

Mindfulness is a mainstream activity now, but at that time it was a departure from my norms. I'd mostly lived on Autopilot. Mindfulness is meditation-on-the-go, paying attention to the present moment without dissecting it or judging it as good or bad. It includes noticing your sensory experience - what you see, taste, touch, hear, smell - and noticing how thoughts, emotions and impulses come and go without having to hitch a ride on them. Mindfulness doesn't mean being cheery all the time. Before it was called mindfulness it was called "Attention Training" which is less trendy but more accurate and probably more useful. Mindfulness bridges the mind and body, thinking and being, strengthening your awareness of being here.

The mindfulness meditation class was on a Tuesday evening in a village hall on a single track lane out of reach of SatNav. Meditation wasn't my thing at all but I had to do something differently. I had driven down the lane twice before in my life: once to visit my mum in a nearby hospital after a failed attempt to claim her body back from ovarian cancer; the other to visit premises for a quick operation which all but guaranteed I would have no more children. Driving down the lane again to my virgin meditation class, further than I had ever been, I passed both premises I had previously visited and winced.

The old door jammed a little on the threshold, revealing scuff marks from all the historic efforts of people trying to get into the place. Or out. Three heaters with a single orange bar hung from each side of the apex ceiling like stadium floodlights on snooze. Twenty people stood in non-linear patterns, nearly all men, smiling and nodding at each other, readying themselves. We migrated to a circle of upright plastic chairs. For the next hour, after some basic instruction, we breathed and counted. Breathed, and counted, all the way up to ten. This was nursery school for the mind. Learning mindfulness meditation is like learning to swim: it's important to start at the shallow end with your feet firmly on the ground. The teacher introduced us to the term "prapanca" meaning "thoughts bouncing off more thoughts", as the mind spins off into abstractions, fantasies, negative forecasts and worry. "What if...? But then what if...? And then what if...?" Thinking can become a bottomless pit of investigation. "Thoughts are like rabbits", wrote author Graham Greene, "they just go on breeding."

The breath is always and only in the present. We can't do yesterday's breathing or add extra breaths to next Thursday. The discursive-thinking mind will always yo-yo between past and future, between rehearsing what was and worrying about what's next, that's how it works and what it's obsessed with. Breathing is only here and now. You can't leave your breathing behind. The dog won't eat it (hopefully). Your breath won't betray you. This makes breathing a useful anchor to bring ourselves back to where we are whenever *prapanca* takes hold. When we inhabit this "now" it becomes less empty. Our thoughts trick us into thinking something is always missing but meditation helps us locate the "it". We are the "it". When we come back to our own presence we tap into our intrinsic resources, our compassion, openness and shared humanity. It's all there all along.

Meditation has gained a solid scientific base over the last 30 years with evidence of its practice reducing levels of stress hormones (cortisol), lowering the risk of high blood pressure and heart disease, and increasing feelings of equanimity. Research by Dr. Norman E. Rosenthal, who has studied mental health for nearly four decades, shows regular meditative practice has not only physical health benefits but changes the way we experience distress, enlarging our capacity to cope effectively. Regular practice (around 10 minutes a day, several times a week for three months or more) shrinks the two almond-shaped amygdala at the core of our limbic brain (the part which reacts with fight, flight, freeze and fog). Conversely, the prefrontal cortex (the HQ for our analysing, planning, calculating functions), increases in capacity. The effect of this is good news: we learn to take a breather rather than react based on old, automatic programming. This equanimity - a glowing sense that all will be well - brings greater focus, creativity, courage and inspiration. We become less distracted by the "breeding rabbits" in our minds and get more traction with reality.

Occasionally our teacher (who has the squeakiest chair) encourages us to scan our body parts to check they are still in the room. "Bring your attention to your ears" the teacher says, "now bring your attention to the tip of your nose". He seems keen on taking our attention to the peripheral parts. I mentally scan every part of my body and feel relief that it's all there. Sometimes I open one eye to check the room when everyone else has their eyes closed. One guy with unbrushed hair wiggles his nose as if desperately trying not to pick it; another in a lumberjack shirt scratches his crotch like he is plunging a sink. I assume he is enjoying his object of meditation. A young lady with an egg-shaped face scowls as if hunting for all her thoughts which have disappeared. I liked these people a lot, they were normal, truthful, and none of them knew me. I liked that we didn't have to sing or pretend we were having spiritual orgasms. We sat in a poorly-lit village hall practising how to come back to earth. I carried on with the meditation class for over two years. Breathing slowly and counting each breath arriving, then leaving, arriving, then leaving. It helped me act less like Orion the hunter, always in chase of some unattainable ideal. Sitting still helped me reconcile to a long list of what I had loved and lost. Instead of avoiding the grief, I came to befriend it.

There is a danger with mindfulness when it gets used as an excuse to split off a part of ourselves away from hurts, worries or fears we don't want to face. "Balloon mindfulness" I call it, the floaty nonsense that says "up, up and away! I'm free!". Mindfulness is not an emotional anaesthetic. We shouldn't encourage people to put a mindful smile on their pain. Believing you're some super-awake guru because you're into mindfulness and meditation is just another game the ego plays. Mindfulness practice, true practice, needs to be tethered to reality and reality is often uncomfortable, "okay, this is happening, stay with the trouble, don't flip out". B r e a t h e. Paradoxically, practising being at ease in the present requires intentional effort. Research indicates mindfulness is particularly effective when linked to talking therapy (such as cognitive-behavioural or person-centred counselling), so the "breathing, counting, noticing" behaviours can work symbiotically with the "processing and understanding" behaviours located in different parts of the brain. Once we've learned to sit still, we can turn our attention to our true intentions and allow a new narrative of who we are becoming in the world to emerge. Until we slow down and sit sill, there's no chance.

Poet Gerard Manley Hopkins called it our "inscape", being aware of what's going on inside ourselves, being in touch with the interior landscape of our motives and moods. Becoming aware of our own edges. Our capacity to remain in contact with the process of life, especially getting through times of confusion and difficulty, requires a kind of backward effort. Learning to *not* do something is sometimes harder than learning to do it. Adapting from "who you used to be" towards "who you are *becoming*" is not a process mapped with rings at your core, like trees, or stratified by lines on a cliff face. The map of your own development is subjective, but not illusory. "Backward effort" means checking in with your all-too-familiar impulses (to act out, avoid pain, fantasise, be suspicious, criticise and so on), yielding for a moment before responding. Mindfulness helps us pause so we don't disappear down holes in the dark and create unnecessary drama.

I clambered out of the manhole I had fallen down that night, with bruised shins and grazed palms. Jess, who witnessed me disappear in the twilight, helped drag the manhole cover back over the hole, making the ground safe again. Having ushered the bin back into its rightful place, we collapsed into laughter, because that's all you can do when you come back to yourself.

I don't recall running the last 6.6 mile loop along the Jurassic Coast, but somehow I did. "Disassociation", psychologists call it, a mental occupation strategy where the mind flees from reality and entertains itself with ideas and imaginings to get away from pain. In endurance events this is common and often effective, until the pain catches up with you later.

The final 200 metre descent onto the shingle beach is painful. There is no crowd cheering us on, no painted banners with exclamation marks to make us feel like heroes. Just the loud crunch of shingle shifting beneath tired feet. The beach leads to the lane, the lane to the field, the field to the puttering race flags and the flags to the inflatable arch of the finish line. I cross the line feeling spent. The wooden medal each runner receives has the face of T-Rex on it (the dinosaur, not the 1970s rock band), plus a pair of striped bamboo socks and a reusable coffee cup.

Reclining in a deck chair by the finish soaking in the sun, the lady with double blonde plaits I was chasing half an hour earlier stands in front of me. Her shadow cools my skin. "What got you into running?" I ask her. "It was after my divorce" she says, "but it's hard fitting in training runs because one of my sons has Down's syndrome and another son, well, his heart stopped beating at a year old and he nearly drowned in the bath. It's a full time job being a single mum". Today's marathon was part of her training to do a 50 mile ultra marathon in the Brecon Beacons in a few weeks time. I sit in quiet awe at her determination to transmute trauma into triumph. "I was reading a book before the race today" she says, leaning down to stretch out her right calf, plaits dangling over her shoulder. "It was about the problems ultra-distance runners face and how they overcome them." Now she is lower I have to shield my eyes from the sun. "Basically" she says, bending with hands on hips, "you have to learn how not to puke up even though you feel like puking for a hundred miles", and we both laugh before walking back through trampled nettles to the car park.

From my tent on the cliff top I watch the sea rush in, then retreat. Herring gulls cry. As the sunlight disappears, I realise where I need to run next: a place of caves and facing fears.

CHEDDAR GORGE

When stuck, breathe

Next to the trolley shelter in the supermarket car park stands a parking warden, her face dotted with sweat and dressed for combat. She lingers, ready to ambush if I don't walk directly from my car to the ticket machine. It's too stifling to get changed into running kit inside the car, so the busy car park with its festival of clanking trolleys and gossiping shoppers rushing for groceries will have to do. The warden, soldered to the spot, stares at me as I peel off each layer of clothing, perhaps expecting me to streak naked. She relents as I walk to the ticket machine looking like a runner rather than a streaker. The machine is scorching to touch and the screen impossible to read in the glare. My debit card jams in the slot, so I fear I may have paid for lifetime parking. I have arrived, but may never leave.

Cheddar Gorge was formed during the ice ages over a period of more than half a million years when permafrost blocked the caves causing the limestone to become impermeable. When the ice and mud thawed during warmer periods, river water dissolved the limestone rock creating cathedral-like caverns, spiked with stalactites and stalagmites.

Water was thrust to the surface sculpting the gorge.

In 1903, Britain's oldest complete human skeleton, Cheddar Man, was found near here, reportedly buried in a special place in the cave to stop his spirit passing to the land of the ancestors. Estimates date the skeleton at over 9,000 years old which is a long time to be waiting in the Final Departure Lounge. It was here, 30 years ago, I got perilously stuck in a cave whilst on a scouting trip. Perhaps this is why I have returned to Cheddar Gorge, why this place made the cut and became a Fat Red Dot on the map at home.

Spreading the map across the open car boot, I plot three different running loops, each roughly nine miles. The first loop ascends the gorge to the east; the second circuits Cheddar reservoir to the west; the third loops around Batts Coombe Quarry to the north of Cheddar village. The map feels smooth, but the true terrain will be different.

After running for two miles looking for a path onto the grassland slopes, I realise I have passed the same nest of thatched cottages three times. Each roof roasts in the sun like burnt toast. I wonder if Cheddar Man also had this problem with navigation. Cheddar is not an easy place from which to escape. I fear being left to rot somewhere along Hannay Road, a pair of decaying fluorescent trail shoes being the only remains found in 9,000 years time.

In the heart of the village I turn up Redcliffe Street and after a short ascent, find a five-bar metal gate leading onto a narrow path. The latch scrapes then clunks, echoing behind me like the closing of a prison cell door. On the path ahead, dozens of tree roots jut up from the path like half-buried human bones. Cow parsley spills across the path under a canopy of broadleaf trees, creating polka-dot sunlight to run through, welcome temporary shade. A blue arrow on the next gate indicates, finally, the West Mendip Way, opening onto the Mendip Hills. Each step further up and further out leads to an expanding perspective. I turn and see the giant blue circle of the reservoir sitting to the west, between the villages of Axbridge and Cheddar. Further south, Nyeland Hill rises like the crooked knuckle of an index finger. With this wider lens view, looking over the place from which I have finally got free, my body relaxes, enlarges even. As cloud-cover shifts, the gleaming eye of the reservoir reflects bright light, then darkens, before light returns, as if the reservoir is winking. All this was here before me and will be here after I am gone

Whereas in the supermarket car park, the pace was frenetic as trolley wheels clamoured for pole position, by contrast here there is just ease. "Ease is a presence defined by an absence" says Nancy Kline, a pioneer in researching the conditions in which people do their best thinking. An absence of tension, competition and urgency, or even an absence of Absence. "Ease recedes but is easily retrieved" she says, "helping us see what is simply true." Ease, I guess that's what rescued me when snagged in the cave as a teenager three decades ago.

What happened was this: The rest of the scout group had continued further on into the cave, but my harness snagged whilst squeezing between two caverns. I became wedged, like a doorstop, in a limestone vice. The qualified instructor behind me, in the cavern I had only half-escaped, murmured advice both urgent and vital, but I could neither see nor hear him. Laying prostrate in the cave, the head torch illuminated a two inch circle. I kissed the cave floor each time I turned my head. My arms were pinned by my side. I could not move forward and I could not go back the way I came. The gravity of the world pressed down. Breathing accelerated. After half an hour, with the fear and instructor's voice crescendoing, and with a ferocious headache, some ancient instinct took hold. My body softened, totally yielding, as if all the fear had bubbled to the surface and was now dissolving into the earthen coffin in which I was buried. Something gave. I wriggled into the next cavern, a torn jacket and grazed skin a small price, and entered a space only a little larger than the one before. But I could breathe again. I could bloody well breathe! And every breath was a gift.

Running through Bubwith Acres Nature Reserve I am on the lookout for ravens and peregrine falcon nesting nearby. Gorse bushes blaze with coconut-scented flowers, hawthorns pour white petals Niagara-like to the floor. The gorge is rich in biodiversity: dormice, yellow-necked mice, slowworms, adders, plus rare butterflies including dingy skipper and the lazily named large blue butterfly all reside here. I wonder, *what am I to them?* An imposter, observer, hunter, guest? "Kiss the earth with your feet" said Tibetan monk Thich Nhat Hahn. I wonder what effect my footsteps have on eco-systems invisible to human eyes. Harebells quiver either side of the path, a wildflower notable for its purple-blue bell-shaped head. Clumps of white-flowering pignut, a member of the carrot family, fan outwards from the earth like open hands. Their tubers, I later learn, are edible and taste like hazelnuts. Each footstep unleashes incalculable consequences.

The hill steepens. I pump arms, lift knees, drop my chin in a posture of defiance, until I come face to face with a horse and its foal glaring at me over a barbed wire fence within breath-smelling distance. We eye-ball one another until I sneak through a gap in a dry-stone wall from which tiny blue faces of germander speedwell peek out. The walls are a typical feature of the Mendip landscape from the field enclosures of the 19th century. Huge sections of wall have collapsed, boulders the size of footballs hurled across the fields, as if a giant has barged his way through. Gangs of cowslip, so-called from "cow-slop" or "cow-dung", bow their tiny egg-yolk heads to the ground like searchlights, as if inspecting the dirt from which they have miraculously emerged.

Straying from the West Mendip Way, I cut through the hundred acres of Middledown nature reserve and find an exit onto Middle Down Drove. The bulk of a 4 x 4 vehicle splattered with mud blocks the way. Time to breathe in, squeeeeeeeze past, keep running. Walls spidered in moss line an unpaved road, a type of lane known in northern England as a "twitchel" or "fork in the road". Leaping the puddles which swell in the track, the run finds its own rhythm. Earth absorbs the body. In the supermarket car park I peeled off layers of clothing, but here I discard layers of thought. The Celtic saints talked about "thin places", specific geographies on the map where the sacred could be felt more keenly. I wonder if those places ever got marked as Fat Red Dots.

I feel a lightness of being, a euphoria, a warmth originating not from the head, but the heart. Euphoria is different to happiness. It comes from the Greek *euphoros* meaning "healthy", or "ability to endure easily" and was used in the 18th century to describe relief from drugs. Neuroscientists tell us that enjoyable times in nature can have a euphoric, calming effect on the amygdala, deep in our reptilian brain. As we go further out into spaces not colonised by humans, away from rattling trolleys, shoppers and menacing parking wardens, something else presses into us. The bouldered walls erected between our interior self and exterior world collapse. We feel differently because we think differently. We think differently because we are in a larger space. Like limestone, we become permeable, and life flows through us easily.

At the hill-crest a solitary buzzard dips in muted flight and a glider simultaneously hums into view. Each looks like a giant X in the sky, seeking a place to land. All three of us - bird, machine and human - are in motion, in flight from one place in search of another, ready to plummet and land. I fling my arms out to form an **X** in a gesture of comradeship with the buzzard and aircraft, not sure if I am sending a massive kiss or offering myself as target practice.

Reaching the junction of the B3135 and B3371, an ice cream van snoozes in the lay-by. As I sit on the stone wall to check the map, a camper van reverses within inches of my toes. The driver has their hands full, holding a cone with a flake in each hand. On the map, the B3135 looks like it twists through the heart of the gorge, through its deepest cut at 449 feet. Just over 50 years ago the gorge flooded and the force of water pushed large boulders down this road, damaging a café and, sweeping cars away.

I begin the descent, crossing the narrow S of the road from side to side, pressing against sharp-fingered hazel, rowan, sycamore, letting cars pass me at the blind bends, curving my body so I become sculpted by the gorge. In lulls between the gush of traffic, blackbirds sing. Then a van swerves toward me as if taking aim. I grasp the nearest tree for safety, cursing the driver as he speeds past, before remembering *I am the thing which is in the way.* Anxiety rises, so I divert onto a path off the road, climbing into a tightly-knit crop of trees, where huge yews scratch my face. There is the stink of wild garlic. Between rocks swathed in moss, a patch of bluebells are in flower, assembled like a secret gathering. The gap between each yew becomes smaller, until I run hunched, scratched, scraped, squeezed, a gatecrasher to the bluebell party. There seems no path through. I admit defeat, scrambling down the bank of garlic to rejoin the B-road, arriving by chance opposite Black Rock gate where the dry-stone wall has collapsed and there is space to get through. I have to keep going if I am going to complete this marathon before dusk. I find another path up a steep ascent towards Draycott and toe-step from rock to rock all the way to the gorge heights. Primitive goats range across the plain, one has its head stuck in a wire mesh fence and looks confused by how it got there. I scan the wide unfolded landscape, the embodied map, this terrain of being. Dropping the backpack to the ground reminds me of the dead-weight which has been hanging on my shoulders all this time. The backpack thuds onto a vast slab of rock, thousands of years old, upon which someone has graffitied the word "EURO" six times in turquoise bubble lettering. The letters increase in size each time, as if the landscape has become a currency and the rock is protesting louder and louder and louder. "Is anyone listening?" the earth enquires.

At the end of the gorge I run down the steps of Jacob's Ladder which joins the end of the trail to the road and Gough's Cave at the bottom. The staircase name was inspired by the biblical story in Genesis when angels ascended and descended a ladder in Jacob's dream. They would have to be damn fit angels going up and down this staircase. I attempt to count the steps, arriving at the bottom but having forgotten the magic number, I sprint back up, before running down again. On the third attempt I am convinced there are 274 steps each way, then wonder why I obsessed about the numbers so much.

Back at the car in Cheddar village, with just over nine miles complete, I recharge the watch and phone and refill the water bottle. My knees feel full of lactate acid from the ambitious exertions up and down Jacob's Ladder. I place the map in the car boot, its creases peaking and falling like the paused graphic of a heartbeat, then ease it open, little by little. A man approaches, his face obscured by a wide-brim hat and pink-framed sunglasses. "Have you been running?" he asks. I snort at his powers of deduction. He tells me about when he ran a fell race in the Lake District and the disgust, present in his tone of voice, that "there was no water station at the top of the fell". It seems nobody warned him about the disappointment at reaching the top. He wags his index finger at me. "You know my doctor says the human body is not built for marathons". My body sags on the car bumper as he lectures me. His tummy bulges like a molehill causing the cannabis leaf symbol on his t-shirt to protrude. I wonder how selective he is about the medical advice he receives.

Heading towards the reservoir, cow parsley foams onto the lanes and a tortoiseshell butterfly leads the way. At the big blue button of water, I run clockwise. Two common swifts, fresh arrivals from their 600 miles a day migration from Africa, twist past me like black sickles, cutting invisible serrations in the sky. Swifts have been known to reach speeds of over one hundred miles per hour. Their scientific name is "Apus apus", meaning "without feet". Their claws are better designed for snatching than walking. They feed, wash, sleep, mate and gather nest-material whilst in flight, needing no rest. Swifts have an instinct for finding home, returning to their favourite nesting sites each year, not because they are sentimental like humans, but because it is efficient to have a familiar environment for feeding and protecting their young. Two more swifts intersect, joy-riders performing aerial handbrake turns, whistle-like screams guillotining the air. Later this evening they will rise higher where the thinner air is more energy-efficient, allowing almost effortless movement. I cannot keep pace with them and too soon they are gone. The heat is intense. I peel my t-shirt off so as I run around the reservoir it looks like I am waving a white flag of surrender.

By 5.00 p.m., with 17 miles run, most visitors have gone. My northern circuit passes up through The Pinnacles, the tallest peaks in the gorge. Running up the gorge valley, I feel its defiance rising up on either side like closing doors. The D of a half moon climbs in day-blue sky behind them. Rock debris litters the roadside. I look for a peregrine falcon, but only see a gang of crows in flight appearing like nine spades on a playing card. A huge group of young people hang out below the cliffs in various lay-bys along the gorge, gathered around souped-up Ford Fiestas and models of Honda from before they were born. A solitary police car sits amongst them. I pass Lion Rock and Pride Evans hole near to which two bodies are pinned to the rock face, their climbing harnesses tinkling, ropes slapping against rock, echoing through the gorge. Another man hangs perpendicular to the rock, without a helmet, motionless like a mannikin, just gazing into the abyss of the sky.

Black Rock, West Mendip Way, Long Wood, Ashridge Farm. Dots of disparate places become connected as I continue. The sun slips down like a gold coin into a pocket. Seeded dandelion heads hover like a million tiny full moons above the grass waiting to be blown to smithereens. With 22 miles run, at Batts Combe quarry, the descent becomes uneven, the path strewn with disturbed stones. I feel emptied, unclenched. Running down the gorge, as I complete the marathon distance, a police car with its sirens crying chases a Honda from which two teenagers wave middle fingers out of open windows, speeding beneath the massive erect finger of The Pinnacles. Passing the Dreamhunters Centre at the bottom of the gorge, a neanderthal figure is painted in luminous blue on the windows and repeated six times across the glass panes, representing stages of human evolution, from crouching caveman to the final figure - a silhouette who has straightened up, erecting by degrees into a Runner. It is Cheddar Man coming to life, either searching for escape or realising he is free to pursue life beyond the Cave.

SUMMER

"Your integrity is your destiny"

—Heraclitus

I awake at 3.00 a.m. after three hours sleep. The room is coloured indigo. Thoreau described mornings as "the most memorable season of the day" when "some part of us awakes which slumbers all the rest of day and night." This morning it is the part of me that remembers it didn't wash up last nights dishes. Repetitive thoughts have kept me awake, mostly those of a neurotic nature. I shuffle to the kitchen, fill a sink with hot water and scrub the frying pan free of fried egg leftovers. I press my heels into the ground to calm myself, like the mindfulness teacher taught us. At 4.15 a.m. I tiptoe down the four flights of stairs, missing out the step with the broken edge, and walk through the sleeping village to cross the old Saxon bridge built by monks. A single swan glides upon the river, appearing as a super-imposed white S upon the dawn-time mist. I count 21 starlings perching on telephone wires looking like musical notes on a score. It is a two mile walk to Dorothy's Wood. There is no traffic. "All memorable events" wrote Thoreau, "transpire in morning time and in a morning atmosphere." But during these liminal months I have become a creature of the night, an owl not a lark, and this feels as if I am trespassing in foreign territory.

Walking through the field-mist swimming at my ankles, a memory returns: I recall as a 12 year old boy the metallic creaking of the garage door at home as I lifted it to retrieve my bicycle to do a morning newspaper round. My paper round began at 5.45 a.m., something I did every day for four years except Christmas Day. I recall childhood days when there were so many new things to walk into. When life was worth getting up for. The nostalgic past can feel more alive, more tangible and vibrant than the uncertain future. Mist absorbs my feet as I arrive in Dorothy's Wood. In ambering dawn-light I stare at gossamer webs clinging to teasel stems. When the sun appears just before 5.00 a.m. it looks like an orange button. I stare at the sky-fire, light burning onto my eyes, piercing thought and soaking skin. The mind clears. I can't rewind the past. I can't undo that which is already said and done. I can't insert the wisdom of now into the events of back then. The sun burns with brilliant indifference. Looking over my shoulder to check nobody else is around, I stretch out my index finger in front of me, closing one eye to ensure accuracy and aim my finger at the sun, pretending to switch it on as if claiming a future that I know nothing about. Like Copernicus, I sense anew that which life truly revolves around: Love. Love for self; love for others; love for this spinning earthly home. What else matters?

There are places still to run, and dots to join. Yesterday's storms are past, today's energy is needed for whatever comes next. As I return to the flat, the mist has become memory and the starlings have flown. I climb the stairs and begin the ironing, thinking about the next run, a journey across the sea.

MOURNE WAY

Leave the place cleaner than you found it

Shoving open the door with both hands, I step onto the deck and feel my skin immediately stretched and scoured by wind. Gripping the rail, solid bulges of paint become enclosed within my fingers as the ferry judders out from Liverpool Bay, pushing its 20 tonne body across the Irish Sea at 20 knots. Before arriving in Belfast, the coastlines of England, Wales, Scotland, Ireland, Northern Ireland and the Isle of Man may come into view. Sightings of bottlenose and short-beaked common dolphins are also possible, but as the ferry skids over Conwy oil and Morecambe gas fields I look out and all I see is a gas rig, a metallic interruption on the skyline assembled like an indecipherable word:

The Mournes, from the welsh meaning "sea-circle", are a cluster of mountain peaks an hours drive south of Belfast, granite waves frozen in time by the motion of glaciers, 50 million years old. Within this Area of Outstanding Natural Beauty (AONB) rests The Silent Valley reservoir, and across them runs the Mourne Wall, built at the turn of the 20th century. I understand almost nothing of Northern Ireland's history other than what I have been fed on mainstream news over the years, everything framed by terrorism, politics and religion, a "troubled place".

Beneath the waves I spot an inflated white shape swimming alongside the ferry, a plastic carrier bag, its shredded handles wafting in the water like jellyfish legs. This morning, whilst waiting to board the ferry, scientists discussed on the radio how the oceans - which produce half the air we breathe - are saturated with more than five trillion pieces of plastic, suffocating marine life. I picture the number: 5,000,000,000,000. So many zeroes, like the open mouths of fish or the closed eyes of humanity. Seahorses cling to disposable cotton buds. Whales digest discarded carrier bags on a diet of five a day. Scientists from Malaysia and France have discovered micro-particles of nylon, polystyrene and polyethylene in various types of fish, including mackerel and anchovies, warning that as plastic attracts toxins in the environment, these poisons could be released into the human body after eating the fish. A plastic bag sits at the base of the Mariana Trench, the deepest oceanic trench on earth. Leaning on the railing, I watch a northern gannet launch off the sea-skin, its black wing-tips looking like they have been dunked in oil.

As the plastic bag floats past, a fog of cannabis spreads across the ferry deck. A man in a blue tracksuit stands at the rail, pinching a spliff so his hand makes the gesture for "okay". His feet point inwards like two shy lovers. I move to the other side of him so I am not downstream of the smell and keep staring at the water. Another white shape appears in the sea, this time it is a real jellyfish, probably a barrel jellyfish given its ghost-white colour and length of around 70 centimetres. I gasp but nobody else shows interest. Its tentacles mimic the handles of the plastic bag, waving like a magician attempting to conjure something from a top hat. I wonder if the two ghosts - one plastic, one marine - will soon meet, like a disastrous blind date. Everything is not okay. The ferry journey is eight hours so I attempt to sleep on a canteen chair, hypnotised by the guttural groan of the ferry dragging us from one port to another, my head swimming in plastic, cannabis, the cry of gulls. I ache. Not just in my bones, but something deeper, as if caught between what's gone and what's not yet come.

A confession: I didn't camp. I blew the budget on a decent Bed and Breakfast on Dougans Road in Kilkeel, negotiating a double helping of porridge for race day shortly after dawn.

A cobweb clings to the wing mirror as I drive down The Mourne Coastal Road. The road snakes and is coiled with blind spots. Badly painted wooden signs dangle from telegraph poles on the bends, each sign hung like a dying body upon a crucifix. The biblical messages oscillate between hope ("Today is the day of salvation") and judgement ("The Wages of Sin is Death"), as if God has attachment issues. I imagine the psychoanalyst Sigmund Freud interviewing God on his therapeutic couch: "Where does this almighty anger come from, God? Who is it for? Tell me about your relationship with your father..."

In the field at Kilbroney Park near Rostrevor the car squelches to a stop, alongside two other cars. Stepping out the car, both my ankles are immediately swallowed by mud. Collecting a race number from the marquee a lady reveals the real start line is in Newcastle, an hour's drive away. We will be transported there by minibus. I wait in my car as drizzle settles on the windscreen like a gathering of full stops, breeding in number until the whole screen looks shattered, like a broken lens.

Rain pelts the minibus as we skirt Carlingford Lough, as if the tempest wants to get at us before we even begin the run. The runner sat next to me is a policeman who has just come off his night shift and hasn't yet slept. "I've done this race a few times", he sniffs, making a clicking noise with his throat, as if he wants to spit something out, "it's effing brutal" he says. Today is NOT the day of salvation. We are entering hell.

By the time we reach Donard Park the rain has slowed. Two hundred runners assemble at the start line - an unmarked path next to a yellow litter bin. One man pushes against a nearby sycamore tree, head down, as if the challenge to come is personified: Man vs. Nature. Another runner stands in a teapot pose, balancing on one leg. Another is on tip-toes, his muscly arms speared upwards, biceps inked with snake tattoos but body poised like a ballerina ready to twirl. I wait beneath an oak tree whose branches sag with the weight of the morning downpour, wondering if my perception is a hangover from yesterday's exposure to marijuana.

The terrain for the run, according to the race director, will be "a bit of everything": marshland, stone paths, stream-crossings, woodland, mud, paved roads, scree. "Your task today" he says, "is to leave the mountain cleaner than you found it". Mutual shouting begins, a countdown from ten, nine, eight… Watches bleep in unison, a crescendo of beginnings, and the human pack of blue tattoos, fluorescent t-shirts and wobbly flesh, surges forward. The centripetal force that gathered us at the point of genesis shifts to a centrifugal energy, unleashing the physical mass up the hill into Tollymore Forest Park. Woodland which has breathed for over 200 years, now heavily populated with invasive rhododendrons, receives us. Today runners become the new invaders, faces flushed like rhododendrons in bloom, 400 feet pummelling the ground, thumping the mountain. A torrent of white-water thrusts itself down rocks. I stop and stare at the waterfall, listening to its ancient conversation and watching its white tongue curl and carve, urging its way down, as if searching for something lost. When I look back, everyone has disappeared so I am last.

The climb continues, brushing past gorse bushes, before a series of stiles six feet high. I see runners ahead keeping to single file, hopping from rock to rock trying not to twist an ankle. The forest has been significantly hacked away here, Scots Pine scattered like matchsticks dropped from height. Mist hangs like lace over Dundrum Bay to the right.

I can't stand it anymore. I spot a runner ahead dropping energy gel wrappers and a plastic bottle onto the woodland track. My fuse is lit. Someone should nail a sign to a nearby tree "The Wages of Littering is Death". I pick up their dented two litre water bottle cast to the side of the track and repeatedly club it across my left palm, until the dent disappears. It is a gesture of intent, declaring warfare with the reclaimed bottle as my weapon of choice. When plastics and non-natural rubbish decompose (which can take 500 years), vulnerable chemicals leek into the eco-system. Small animals can easily become trapped in cans and bottles, or plastic tags get stuck in their throats. RAGE! That's what I feel, so I shout at the group of runners in front: "When you chuck your rubbish into the forest, what do you think is going to happen to it? Are you expecting your mother to clean up after you?" One of them glances over their shoulder, then replies, something about being a "tosser", which is ironic given who threw the litter.

Emotions don't follow tidy linear sequences. If we deny, suppress or avoid our emotions, especially strongly-felt ones, they just leak out elsewhere in our behaviour. Emotions need noticing, naming and using in a constructive way. As the work of grief expert Elisabeth Kübler-Ross reminds us, feeling angry is not bad or wrong, anger is a grief emotion, part of an inevitable chain reaction to loss. Anger (resentment, fury, rage) is a protective emotion, a visceral clue as to where our values hide. I wish I had understood that earlier in life instead of believing that anger was a scary emotion to stay away from. Anger is no excuse for aggression. Anger in its various forms is an attempt to get back what matters, giving us energy to act and a voice to be heard. There's more going on here than a subjective reaction to some litter. The rage points to the devastating losses going on all around us. Australian philosopher Glenn Albrecht and his research team coined the grief-related term "solastalgia" to describe "the distress... produced by environmental change impacting on people while they are directly connected to their home environment". Albrecht continues, "the negative effect...is exacerbated by a sense of powerlessness or lack of control over the unfolding change process." If you're not feeling the rage of how collectively we are suffocating the planet with our waste, then you're probably on a different planet.

For the next four miles I run, halt, collect whatever rubbish I see and stuff it into the plastic bottle. When the first bottle becomes full I find another (should it be this easy?) and begin the process again. Run, halt, pick up, stuff it in. Another runner joins me in silently collecting litter. Then another, as if cleaning up the place is contagious. We don't speak as we do this, as if in mourning. Protruding from a hole in the trunk of a beautiful oak tree, a plastic carrier bag bulges with empty sweet packets, as if someone has tried to stuff its gob. I snatch the bag from the tree-mouth, choking on expletives. In the heart of the wood, the marathon route crosses Spinkwee River where eight flat rocks, like enormous piano keys, provide a way across. Once my companions have crossed, I leap onto the first rock, a two litre plastic bottle full of litter balanced in each hand like the scales of justice.

"Locard's exchange principle", named after French criminologist Dr. Edmond Locard, acts as the basis of all forensic science. The principle states that "every contact leaves a trace". The criminal will bring something into the crime scene and leave with something from it. "Wherever he steps, whatever he touches" writes criminologist Paul Kirk, "whatever he leaves, even unconsciously, will serve as a silent witness against him". For the criminal this might include hair, fibres from clothes, tools liable to scratch surfaces, human fluids. They all "bear mute witness" says Kirk. "This is evidence which doesn't forget. It is not absent because human witnesses are absent. It is factual…only human failure to find, study and understand it can diminish its value."

Locard's exchange principle is not confined to crime scenes but is embedded in all the systems in which we participate. Our lives imprint upon the environment, and the environment imprints upon us. Today we were tasked with leaving these mountains "cleaner than we found them". Research in the field of positive psychology shows how litter picking has a beneficial impact, not only on the environment, but also boosts levels of dopamine and opioids in the brain. There is an exchange happening, a symbiosis we cannot escape. Cleaning up the environment has significant benefits for both individual and collective mental health, the two issues are intricately connected. In my local village, a group called "Rubbish Friends" organise regular clean ups and have diverted over 2000 spectacles cases from landfill via a well known high street store. They regularly pull supermarket trolleys, fish tanks and traffic bollards from local streams. Recovery is not about an individual feeling better about themselves. Recovery includes all of us recovering what truly matters in our time here. *What do you stand for? What are you contributing to others around you? How will you be remembered?*

The principle also extends to our interactions with one another. The week after my marriage ended I sat upon a car park wall, my face turned towards the sun, waiting for something I can't remember. An elderly man, perhaps 80 years old, walked across the car park. He planted his walking stick in front of him and peered at me. "Young man", he said, "you look…you look sad?" I was pulled from my thoughts as I felt the force of being seen. "I am" I said to him, "yes I am. Thank you". That moment was a tiny turning point in a long arc of tiny turning points. That brief, unexpected contact leaves a trace within me still, now scribed upon this page, a moment of truth from a stranger in a story he knows nothing about. I remember him. Kindness endures.

The running checkpoint sits in the shadow of sycamore trees. I hand over the litter-crammed bottles to the race marshal whose facial expression says "what on earth?". Each bottle brims with dry twists of satsuma skin, ripped energy gel wrappers (from today's race), distorted shapes of chewed gum, lollipop wrappers, crisp packets (mostly salt and vinegar), scrunched aluminium foil and in one of the bottles something resembling half a condom, definitely used. In addition, I handover a five minute rant to other runners at the checkpoint based on "leaving the place cleaner than you found it". Anger is protective, aggression is destructive.

As a group of us head towards Fofanny Reservoir together, up a marshy hill which soaks our feet, there's a sudden movement in the grass. I spot a common frog squatting by my toes as if standing guard. It is clearly his mountain too. Reaching the hilltop there's a stream thriving with a dozen frogs, clambering awkwardly over one another, not too dissimilar to the weary runners just ahead negotiating the stile onto Slievenaman Road. One frog wrestles its way over an empty biscuit box next to which are three large ribbed plastic bottles. I leave the frogs, but collect the bottles. The road weaves through a stunning landscape, verdant and angular. At the roadside is a near-constant supply of empty aluminium cans (some with graphically designed animal claws streaking down them) and polystyrene chip packets abandoned like open oyster shells. As my arms become full, a man shouts at me. "Hey, mate, you look like a bloody wheelie bin!" Another runner in a vest laughs as I overtake him. But then he yells after me, "Hey, let us help" and he and two other runners ask to share the load. *Every contact leaves a trace.* Each of them start bending and scooping up litter, each filling a plastic bottle of rubbish. We arrive together at Spelga Reservoir checkpoint with 14 miles run. In exchange for the litter collected there is cake. Lots of cake.

The route towards the finish leads us down Kilkeel Road, across streams where water runs the colour of copper, zig-zagging across marshland under the nose of Hen Mountain and Little Cock Tor (perhaps named after the chap who littered the woods earlier). With 10 miles to go, we traverse and sink down black-peat holes, freezing for the feet, never sure if the next footstep will land on a mound of grass or plunge us down again to the knee. We run parallel to Rocky River, cutting like a blade through the mountain-scape of Tormanrock and Rocky Mountain, its foothills littered with rocks the size of armchairs, before ascending hills purpled with heather. "This is it!" I hear myself say, breathing in the magnificent views, rage becoming peace. At 21 miles, clouds give way to ferocious sunshine, and my watch screen goes blank as if time has run out.

The final three miles through Rostrevor Forest were my fastest of the day. Energy came from somewhere, as if the mountains picked me up like discarded litter and carried me to the finish line. Running felt almost effortless. That night, sore all over, the cold metal of the medal presses upon my chest as I fall asleep, another symbol of extraction from the environment.

In Belfast, before getting the ferry home, I meet John Hill, whom I know from contact on social media. We shake hands in a car park somewhere between the Cathedral Quarter and the Holylands (so named because of the street names, Jerusalem St., Damascus St. and so on) then walk to a café. "A short drive that way" John says "is Cypress Avenue, the inspiration for the Van Morrison song", waggling his finger. It is Sunday morning and families dressed in Sunday best parade on different sides of the street, entering either The Moravian Church of Ireland, The Crescent Church or the Belfast Church of Christ. There's no shortage of choice. Exterior walls of nearby buildings are graffitied with bible verses like those on The Mourne Coastal Road. John oozes a gentleness which I learn, over noodles, he has won through what he has lost. He explains some Belfast history to me, 99 years on from the Government of Ireland Act which brought the partition of Northern Ireland. "It is a fragile peace, the tension is always there" he says. He asks how yesterday's run went. I thank him for introducing me to the Mournes which I had never heard of until I saw his photographs online. "The Mournes" John says, leaning back in his chair and glancing out the window, "I find them unifying". "When you're up in the mountains you meet people from all over the place. I met someone from Tipperary recently" and he shakes his head. "You don't talk politics or religion up there, you just have this thing in common: the mountain." We finish our noodles. "Fancy a trip to Stormont?" he asks.

The imposing Stormont building in Belfast, home to the Northern Ireland Assembly, was designed by architect Sir Arnold Thornely with perfect symmetry and symbolism in mind: the building is 365 feet wide representing one foot for each day of the year, the pillars representing the six counties of Northern Ireland. John tells me about the impact of the Brexit vote in 2016 and that it might urge Ireland towards reunification. We stand on the path looking towards Stormont under a black lamppost. "Nothing takes places in that building" John says, "there's no talking, which means there is no listening either". Heavy rain explodes onto the path like gunfire. Black umbrellas shoot up around us and bodies move with urgency. With no cover we sprint down the driveway as Stormont becomes overshadowed by storm clouds.

Before catching the overnight return ferry to Liverpool, I drive to Strangford Lough and stand gazing at it for two hours. A year from now, during the first pandemic lockdown, orca whales will stray into these inland waters. Sunlight touches the mound on which I stand, creating a halo effect on my feet. A rainbow emerges as if from the lough, launching toward the sky, curling then fading, before continuing a hand span further on, then fading again, before a third vivid burst of stripes. It is a stuttering sign in the heavens written in rainbow morse code, like hope under construction. I need all the encouragement I can find ahead of the next run, the most challenging yet.

MOUNT SNOWDON

You are the mountain you conquer

The ground is too hard for tent pegs so the guy ropes are looped around rocks the size of bread loaves. The map covers the tent floor, a paper carpet upon which hundreds of ascents and descents are printed in two-dimensional form. I have a 1962 edition of this map which reeks of old bookshops, printed in one inch scale with the price of Seven Shillings & Sixpence Net printed on the cover. Contrasting the old and new maps at home revealed little change to the urban, forested or mountainous areas. The stark difference was how the new map is tattooed with blue icons across the surface: public toilets; parking; viewpoints; campsites; fishing areas; golf courses; picnic sites; public houses; stars for tourist features. In exchange, the old map, icon-free, shows submarine contours for the llyns, measured in fathoms, gleaned from admiralty surveys. One map is preoccupied with the surface, the other with depth.

My index finger traces contours, paths, streams. The map is mostly pale yellow, indicating the absence of civilisation, with several A-roads cracking across the map like veins across a palm. I measure in hand spans different ways to run 26.2 miles. The route needs to be safe, circular and scenic, in that order, and it makes sense to reach the summit of Snowdon before heat seizes the day. There will still be 20 miles to run once at the peak.

The English name for Snowdon simply means "snow dune", probably from the Saxon, but the Welsh name has legend attached: Yr Wyddfa, pronounced "er with-va", means "grave" and comes from the legend of the Welsh giant king, Rhita Gawr, who is said to have conquered 30 kings, creating a cloak from their beards which fell from the giant's shoulder to the floor. The legend says the giant lays buried beneath a stone cairn on the mountain summit.

The forecast is a clean blue sky, all day, but conditions at the summit can be in sharp contrast to those in the valley. I intend to begin along the Miner's Track, passing tiny Llyn Teryn (meaning Lake of the Tyrant) next to which lie the crumbled remains of miners' barracks. The track continues over a causeway, crossing Llyn Llydaw, and a short distance beyond there is a disused copper mine. The Miner's Track is wide and flat for the first three miles before converging into the rock-strewn scree-slopes of the Pyg Track. It then zig-zags up to Bwlch Glas and onto the summit itself, 1085 metres above sea level.

My finger halts on the map where the dotted track-line resembles a shark fin. This represents more than a tight physical turning point. The "fin" is as far as I made it on my only previous attempt to climb Snowdon. My finger presses on the co-ordinates, like a bruise, locating vulnerability. There's a pulse of fear as memory returns, an osmosis from map to mind.

Two years ago I was the sole adult in charge of four children climbing the mountain, between the ages of six and twelve. I didn't know about the more accessible Llanberis path to the summit then and assumed, wrongly and foolishly, there was only one way up. I cannot fathom how this detail passed me by. The five of us began on a bright April day walking the Miner's Track, carrying rain coats and flapjacks. Just before Bwlch Glas, a short climb from the summit, having navigated the steep sections, the weather tightened. The mountain turned from friend to enemy within minutes as bodies hurtled down, like villagers fleeing a fire. I am a good runner but a poor climber. Heights frighten me. "It's not very far now Uncle Christopher" my nephew said, who had climbed before in more assured company. All four children looked at me. Stones skidded past our faces in the hurried exit, as if the mountain was sneezing. I looked up. Thick cloud avalanched toward us then closed over us like a hood. We turned and descended as rapidly as possible, surrounded in a fog of anxiety. On the rushed descent, two of the children fell, twisting their ankles. Strangers stopped and helped, giving encouragement, lending shoulders to lean on and sweets to distract them. I know the mountain route until the "fin" turning point. Beyond lies uncertainty. My fingertip probes the map for relief before gliding back down the long green dashes marking the Llanberis path, into the inverted crease of the map where the village of Llanberis waits, as if with open hands. I can replenish my water supply there.

I plan a five mile loop around Llyn Padarn followed by a circuit of Llyn Peris reservoir, amongst the slate quarries and old miner huts. This should get me beyond 20 miles. Once in the valley, I can improvise to reach the marathon mileage. I concertina the map, memory and hope collapsing within. Lulled by the stream-song of the Afon Colwyn next to the tent, I fall into sleep, map still pinched between fingers, resting like a paper butterfly about to take flight.

The birdsong sounds unfamiliar. The tent is cold. Daylight has leaked in since 4.40 a.m. Sleeping in a tent plays havoc with the wake/sleep cycle which helps synchronise us to the normal patterns of the day. The first thing I remember, as tea steams from the flask, is fleeing the mountain two years ago. I unzip the tent and the pull-tab on the zip slider rips off. Getting out the tent becomes an act of escapology.

Driving out from Beddgelert I pass Sygun copper mine where in Roman times tunnels were dug to get to mineral veins deeper in the mountain. Beyond the village two ponies feed in a field at the roadside, nodding their heads as if extolling the new day. For a moment I see an underwater forest, and gasp, before realising it is the reflection of Moel y Dyniewyd in the mirror-like waters of Llyn Dinas. Disorientation: Am I going up or going under?

By 7.00 a.m. Pen-y-Pass car park is full. A lady in a hi-viz jacket signals to continue driving down the road. I reverse park into a lay-by, opposite Cromlech boulders, rocks three times my height, planted like giant fists grasping something with no intention of release. The air is humid, the valley murmurs with traffic. "Morning is when I am awake and there is a dawn in me" wrote Thoreau from his cabin in the woods. Thoreau can sod off. I slouch against my car bumper to eat a bowl of cereal, spoon scraping the metallic dish. Instead of Thoreau's sense of morning majesty I scold myself for forgetting a coat and first aid kit, essential items for ascending a mountain. Complacency. After some rummaging I find an unused foil blanket stuffed in a spare pocket and leftover plasters from running in The Mournes last month. "Just don't fall" I mutter, leaving the empty cereal bowl in the car boot.

It is two miles to Pen-y-Pass, along a winding, rising road, where the Miner's Track begins. Channels of water surge downward through gashes in the mountainside giving it the appearance of a white zip, as if the mountain is undressing. Everyone in Pen-y-Pass car park wears sturdy boots except one young man in flip flops. Across Nant Gwynant valley, Britain's oldest water pipeline rests above the ground looking like a water chute from a theme park. I begin running at a pace under nine minutes per mile, keen to get underway. The path swerves between a dozen black polypropylene sacks, each loaded with a tonne of rocks slung across the track like body bags awaiting mass burial, each rock the size and colour of a skull. None of this helps my anxiety.

Unresolved traumatic experiences - those which have been ignored, denied or played down - can hijack how the brain works, causing us to perceive more people or situations as threatening than is true in reality. Trauma colours the way we see the world. Oftentimes other people and places may be neutral or even healthy and safe for us but past trauma magnifies and intensifies each negative sensation or thought. It is as if we see the world through broken spectacles, not realising it is the lens we look through which is broken, rather than life itself.

When the past interferes with the present we doubt our ability to cope. We archive previous resilience to memory and fool ourselves into thinking we don't know how to handle the challenge before us. Our adjective "anxious" comes from old Latin *angere*, meaning "to choke or squeeze" illuminating the subtle linguistic relationship anxiety has with anger. Both emotions have a "seizing" effect on the brain, tightening the seahorse-shaped hippocampus in the limbic system, interfering with processing thoughts. "I can't think straight" we say, accurately. Anxiety has a certain texture and associates with other names: *shock; worry; panicky; surprise; confusion; overwhelm; bewilderment; puzzled; self-doubt; can't cope; trembly*. The squeeze isn't just in our thinking, it's in the body.

We are on the constant lookout for threat, our own survival becoming priority number one. Dr. Stephen Porges, a leading psychiatrist and neuroscientist in studying trauma, probably best known for The Polyvagal Theory, calls this unconscious scanning "neuroception". Feeling helpless, worried or unsafe, either because of a present threat or echoes of past trauma, triggers the brain's sympathetic branch of the autonomic nervous system, activating the well-known fight or flight response. Feeling anxious is not just a "feeling" but is rooted in key brain and biological processes. Internal chemistry changes. Breathing shallows. Blood pressure increases. Heart rate surges as it pumps blood to the major muscle groups to help with either getting the hell out of there or putting up a fight. Hands and legs tremble ready for action. Sweat bubbles upon skin. Pupils dilate. Shoulders become rigid. The tummy might feel upside down. The throat might feel constricted or a surge of adrenaline might cause a yell. When this occurs, the physical ability to listen shrinks, as stress hormones such as cortisol are released throughout the body. We mislay who we are, where we are, what to do. As distress increases, the brain's dorsal vagal branch becomes active, causing us to freeze up, so we want to hide, curl into a ball, sever eye contact with others. The immune function deteriorates as if in preparation for death. Anxiety causes us to mentally and physically seize up, finding ourselves in two places at once: gravity keeps the body on earth, but the mind rockets into space.

One way of minimising this *prapanca* reaction (the unhelpful multiplication of thoughts) from becoming a choking anxiety is to move from "What if" to "What is". Sense the physical ground through your feet, tune in to the come-and-go of sounds near to you then those which are further away. Breathe down in to the belly, hold the breath there then force a long slow breath out from the mouth. Notice What Is (rather than what isn't). The brain regains oxygen so it can decide what to do next instead of whirring around in a fog. The next step might be asking for help. Feeling grounded improves circulation, digestion, the immune system and expands the range of voice tone. Levels of cortisol recede to healthier levels, and the wellbeing chemicals - oxytocin, opioids, serotonin - all resurrect. The brain's ventral vagus complex and the parasympathetic branch of the autonomic nervous system (ANS) activate physical sensations of calm and ease, enabling a feeling of being settled, able to engage with others more easily and think clearly. It becomes possible to smile and become curious again. We feel the "chemistry" again with where we are, as stable as the mountain.

I reach the causeway where Llyn Llydaw ripples under Snowdon's gaze. The causeway was built in 1853 after a horse drowned pulling copper from the mine on a raft across the lake. To build the causeway, the water level had to be lowered by nearly four metres. In the process of doing so, a pre-historic dug-out canoe, made from oak, was discovered.

A runner appears alongside me, her dark pony tail reaching all the way down her back. "Don't know about you" she says "but I've come here to get away from London", before confessing, "well, away from people actually." Her accent suggests she is from New Zealand. For the next two miles we share running experiences in different parts of the world and advise each other on the best way up the mountain which looks like an immovable capital **A** and whose peak is becoming obscured by cloud, as though its head is being erased. "I know this is a stupid question" she says, as we pass the ruins of the Britannia Copper Mine crushing mill, "but, tell me, which one is Snowdon?"

We mount a brick and boulder path together, which when looking down at it makes you feel like you're running up a wall. At the small loch of Glaslyn a stone plinth indicates where the Miner's Track converges with the Pyg track, two paths becoming one. Quartz rests underfoot. The mountainside is quiet, as if everyone is climbing and inhaling in unison. I ease between rocks, scrambling over boulders half my height. Ponytail Lady sprints ahead as if I am another person to get away from. Then it happens. I reach the shark fin on the map where I turned back with the children two years ago. I recognise the exact rock. Anxiety hijacks. My body temperature plummets, arms grow goose bumps, sweat erupts on my face. I notice the same internal chill as when I hung from the cliff in Tenby. I grip a row of jagged rocks that look like shark teeth. I am about to climb higher on foot than I ever have before and something buried in my brain wants to protect me. There are lots of people here, the weather poses no immediate threat. I know this reaction is not rational, so I hold a conversation between different parts of my brain, like a parent to a child. "Christopher, notice how solid the mountain is beneath your feet. It's okay, yeah? You are NOT going to hurl yourself over the side...are you?" I pause to visualise my body twisting over the mountain edge, arms flapping heavily like the wings of a pterodactyl as I fall, rucksack detaching like unwanted ballast. This is *prapanca* at play again, thoughts breeding thoughts. I grip two fang-like rocks and press both feet down as hard as I can into the mountain. My inner-parent runs out of patience. I just want to get to the top of the mountain, then run down the other side. "Just hold on to the fucking mountain Christopher, okay?" I need an object of focus outside my head to distract me from the mayhem occurring inside. The bare, sunburned legs of an elderly man in front of me will do. Upon his left calf is a scabbed cut in three sections, as if to suggest "cut along the dotted line" and a varicose vein bulges like cauliflower behind his knee. Never before have an old man's legs been so mesmerising but they keep me distracted from imagining my worst case scenario.

Dense cloud spills over the summit, but this isn't the ominous descent of cumulonimbus clouds, just a thick plume of steam from the mountain railway. I slump against a plinth where beneath a circumflex are the words Copa and Summit. The vertical stone points like a finger to the sky. The veil of steam thins and Glaslyn shines below, a lake reduced by perspective to the size of a thumbnail. Snowdonia stretches out like a giant map. The Welsh name for the region of Snowdonia, "Eryri", is believed to originate from the Latin *oriri* meaning "to rise", possibly referring to the Welsh name for eagle, *eryr*. This eagle-eyed view across the landscape offers a feeling of detached ascendency, a sense of "wow-I'm-here" and an intake of breath. Wind flicks at my sweaty running top and I feel the chill. I put on a spare jumper and stuff a silver foil blanket between the layers so as I walk the final few hundred metres up the steps to Snowdon's Trig point to touch the peak, I sound like a crisp packet. I have overcome a fear but there are still 20 miles to run.

At dawn, on a Thursday morning, a few days before attempting Snowdon for the first time with the children, I experienced a strange but beautiful thing. When I awoke my body remained in bed, legs tucked under a freshly-washed duvet, but my awareness was outside of my body and next to the ceiling. I felt the gap between body and mind but couldn't see it. This random out-of-body experience lasted several minutes. It was not a dream, nor my imagination. It was the same difference between asleep and awake, but this was between awake and more-awake. I was somehow in everything, but not my body. I looked across the ceiling, with which I was level, and noticed jagged shapes, like yellow mountain peaks, sunlight casting itself above the drawn curtains. It was like temporary omnipresence, being in two places at once, in the bed and above it. The overwhelming feeling was total peace and I knew, beyond the bones, fibres, atoms of my being, there was nothing to worry about. Worry was No-thing. I had been whisked to an experiential summit, higher than any high I had ever known and it was 100% bliss. There was no fight. No struggle. Just this, and "this" was all. At some point I returned to sleep, falling as if from a great height (I guess my mind fell back into my body) and I had a vivid dream which changed the course of my life at that point, leading me to set up my business a year later. Transcendent experiences are not uncommon, but we don't talk about them because we fear being labelled an oddball.

In the review of General Psychology, David Yaden of the University of Pennsylvania published findings identifying a series of mental states that involve self-transcendence, or "self-loss". Other words given to the experiences included love, awe, mystery, bliss and peak-flow. This seems subjective, but in recent years, a growing consensus of scientists from across the world, including the University of London, have stopped linking "feelings of oneness" with mental illness. "Transient states are marked by decreased feelings of the self, or ego, and increased feelings of connectedness" says Yaden. "Our daily worries can evaporate if we learn to stop and appreciate the majesty of the universe." Thoreau would love this guy. Yaden and his research team cite four "paths to bliss": through spiritual experiences (such as meditating or love-making); connecting closely with nature; having an intense subjective interaction with a work of art or music (like when something "moves" you); and adoration of pure logic, such as that which Einstein described at the laws of the universe.

Five days after this out-of-body encounter, I was clinging to the shark fin on Snowdon as people rushed past, yelling "Get off! Get off the mountain!", my hands trembling, four children staring, questions in their eyes. There was TOTAL worry. Nothing lasts, not even bliss.

I leave Snowdon's summit and follow the Llanberis path down, tip-toeing rock to rock as if on hot coals. Something distracts me, a random *prapanca* moment, thought firing more thought, a memory from out of nowhere of someone who once said something which hurt. I'm caught up in old pain. Separated from the present, my toe stubs on a rock and I trip, as if my angry thoughts have fired a negative pulse into the body of the mountain and the mountain has said "no thanks", rebounding them with force. Both hands slam the scree in front of me as I skid face down like a one man bobsleigh, knees cracking on rock, right shoulder pounding a boulder until I am smeared in white dust and blood runs across both palms in rivulets, like A-roads on a map. I struggle to move. One moment I am on top of the mountain conquering fear, and the next the mountain is on top of me teaching me a lesson.

A man with a bald head, gleaming like a ball of sunlight, stops and lifts me from under my armpits. "Hey, what happened mate?" he says. His voice tone calms me. Another man with sunken cheeks stops by. "Fancy this?" he says, offering a chocolate bar. Sunlight Man takes my hands in his, turning my palms over as if to predict my future. His movements are delicate but purposeful. He pinches the plastic tube to the water pouch on his back, and washes blood from my hands. Water stings the pock marks where gravel has inserted itself beneath skin. I feel shaken. "I...I got distracted" I say, my hands trembling. "I stopped paying attention". There is an audience of five watching this ritual of restoration. Sunlight Man steadies me. "We all fall at some point" he says. He tells me his wife has taken the train to the mountain top, whilst he walks up. "It was our daughters wedding yesterday" he says, and smiles, nodding with the satisfaction of a delighted father. "Your wife will beat you to the top now" I say, in half-apology. He looks to the right where the mountain railway track is visible between ridges, as if dashes of track have been laid but not joined. "It's okay. You learn to not rush things" he says. He removes his glasses to clean them, blinks four times, rapidly, then stretches his eyes wide. I notice his eyes for the first time, dark like vinyl but shining like stars.

The café at the end of the Llanberis path is busy when I arrive sore and shaken. I order a coffee holding my throbbing hands up and apart as if offering the waiter a beach ball. The waiter assumes I mean a large coffee. In the cupboard-sized bathroom, I wash congealed blood from my fingers and wrists, yelping as I do so. When I exit, a queue of people snake back into the seating area, each looking at me with concern as if asking themselves "What the hell was he doing to himself in there?"

Stopping too long will cause the body to seize up so I continue toward Llyn Padarn where a canoe slalom is taking place. Running around the lake then crossing an arch bridge I reach 13.1 miles, precisely halfway. It has taken over three hours. My legs feel heavy from ascending the mountain. My hands sting from the fall. My shoulder feels like it carries the weight of the world.

At the rim of Llyn Padarn I take a few minutes to stand in a mountain pose, feet spread apart, and regulate my breath, feeling entirely conspicuous. Dr. Rollin McCraty at the HeartMath Institute says this is one of the ways we can manage feelings of anxiety and overwhelm. The body is an intrinsically intelligent instrument. Effectively we shift the rhythms of the heart, sending different neural messages to the brain, which McCraty calls "heart coherence". The human heart sends more messages to the brain than the other way around, emanating an electromagnetic field that can be detected up to ten metres away. We know this when we walk into a room and the "vibe" is different, perhaps uneasy, or energised with excitement. We feel it before we understand it.

I run through Fachwen, towards the hamlet of Dinorwig, beneath nests of trees, their branches inter-laced like neural networks. Stopping outside the Lodge café to sort my rucksack, I realise the fall earlier has smashed the lunch box and squashed the food. As I unfold the map like a napkin across my knees, sat on a half-rotted bench, a motorcyclist pulls up next to me and looks at my map. His helmet visor rises an inch. "Mate, hey mate, where are we?" the mouth says. Perhaps the mountain-fall has dazed me. Put on the spot I fail to pinpoint where "we" are and shrug my shoulders. No amount of heart-brain regulation is going to magically improve my orienteering skills. The mouth curses, the visor slams. Motorbike revs c-c-c-c-crack through the quiet valley.

A public footpath takes me past disused miner barracks, slate walls without roofs and pane-less windows. The slate is plagued with scratches, names, dates. One is dated 1908. The barracks remind me of Tintown in the Peak District. I wonder how human life used to thrum here before it moved on. I slide across the slate scree as if surfing over the past. Llyn Peris appears below in the sunshine, the colour of a Caribbean lagoon.

Reaching Llanberis village again, with 19 miles run, there is an ice cream van. My palms throb, the swelling is blue-grey, and my right shoulder feels stiff. I clearly require first aid so I order the largest ice cream with the tallest flake on offer and sit in the sun to enjoy it.

Running along the A4086 back to the car is a slog, past slate heaps as tall as houses, mirroring the mountains from which they were hewn. Through Nant Peris and Gwastadnant I try to stick to ten minute mile pace, but fail. When I reach my car parked by Cromlech boulders, I still have four miles to run. I drop the rucksack and water bottle into the car boot, eat a flapjack (good for glucose) and an overripe banana (for the potassium) before heading off in the direction of Pen-y-Pass for the second time. I want to get this run finished.

Mallory's café sits like a white full stop at the foot of Moel Berfedd ahead, as if the café somehow prevents the mountain from sliding onto the road. I run, keeping the café in sight, but I won't make it up the hill again. Like George Mallory on his first two expeditions to Everest, I turn back, so the last two miles of running are downhill. Sunlight flashes lemon-green through the valley. I feel unfolded beyond the perimeter of skin, as if these are my final breaths, as if I'm giving up my ghosts. "How will you be remembered?" asked Walt Whitman. Perhaps only as one who fell, from the abstract into the specific.

Arriving home the next day after another cold night in the tent, I limp to the map tacked to the wall. By mistake I pick up a purple rather than blue felt-tip pen, so the dot on the map in North Wales turns from red to the colour of deathly nightshade. There are five marathons still to run and everything hurts. The next run is the most weird. A place of vivid dreams, fierce creatures and thunder.

NEW FOREST

We have to get lost to find our way

The thunder sounds like a train approaching. I must keep running. Dense clouds hurl their contents upon the ground. Three wild ponies stare into oblivion, mesmerised by the veil of water rushing from the sky. I shout obscenities, distorting my body beneath, then between, then over fallen tree trunks suspended a few feet off the ground. Finding a way through is like lacing boots. *Why am I attempting this?* I am drenched and tired. It has been five weeks since falling on Snowdon, without a decent run in between time. I froze beneath the stars; collapsed in the Abbey; and fell on the mountain. I worry I will disappear in the forest.

I awoke at 3.24 a.m. with father figures on my mind from a vivid dream. I don't recall previously having a dream featuring my own father before. In the dream, my father, brother and I were jumping on cardboard boxes to collapse them, laughing. Then my brother and I climbed a hill to erect a memorial to my dad. Wide awake and engrossed in figuring out what the dream meant, I unzipped the tent hoping to see a sky constellated with stars like last year with my eldest child. But clouds masked everything. I couldn't get back to sleep so I ate cold porridge and shivered in my sleeping bag. Then the running watch breathed its last digits and went blank forever, so instead of measuring today's run by miles, I set the phone timer for five hours and will run on countdown.

The forest has a strange effect on thinking. Every time I try to follow a path, faithful to some linear way forward, the way is blocked as if the storm has complicated the grammar of the forest so it has become a foreign language. No matter how hard I try to navigate the tangled terrain of bough and branch, the forest shuts me out. An oak tree stands in the stubborn shape of a capital Y, as if it reached a stage in its development where it couldn't decide how to proceed, so it went both ways at once. If only I could split myself into options and explore them simultaneously to see where they end up.

The New Forest in Hampshire is the largest mosaic of unploughed, unsown lowland in Britain and includes 26 miles of coast. Among its ancient deciduous woodland, open grassland, rare wet heathland and bog, is diverse habitat that cannot be found elsewhere. Each autumn 2% of its heathland is burnt to regenerate the heather, which today in wet mid-August, shines like purple gloss. All three types of British snake can be found here, and pigs, cattle and wild ponies all roam free across the area - a reality encountered when putting the tent up yesterday afternoon, when with my back turned, an adult pony entered the tent foraging for breakfast, before attempting to stroll off wearing the tent as a bonnet.

Forests disorientate. They spin us round to see the same things from angles obtuse and acute. Creatures live at all levels, up, down and across. A thousand details thrive at the feet more so than on a street or beach. Squirrels clamber and scurry, hunt and hide, embodying the clandestine buzz of the forest. Forests grasp our senses with their earthy stench and creatures calling in unknown tongues. The forest is never stagnant the way a lake might appear, nor static the way we consider a mountain although all of nature morphs in one way or another. Forests are ancient beyond our understanding. We trespass rather than visit, changed by immersion in their secrets, tested by navigating their labyrinthine paths, as if they unveil who we really are. They are places of oscillation between worlds, between times, between stages of life and states of mind.

Language is our bridge between mind and place. Ten thousand years ago there was no separation between magic, religious myth and medicine, so our present-day vocabulary on mental health draws many associations from both myth and nature. We have "panic" from *Pan*, the Greek god of woods and forests who took people by nasty surprise; and "calm" from *cauma*, the Late Latin for "heat of the mid-day sun" when workers in the Mediterranean took a rest.

In myths and fairytales forests represent an important place on a psychological journey, where naivety branches out into wider awareness. It is usually children who enter the forest to find out who they really are, whether for sanctuary or adventure, and once within the forest are transformed. Hansel and Gretel find their own way into the forest, before getting lost and caught by a witch; Little Red Riding Hood is tricked by the wolf in the forest, who then eats the girl's grandmother for Starters; Sleeping Beauty dozes for a hundred years surrounded by thick forest; and Snow White runs in frightened panic through a forest, away from the huntsman, before finding the home of seven dwarves. It is out in the forest where Rumpelstiltskin dances, singing his true name. The four Pevensie children, Peter, Susan, Edmund and Lucy, penetrate the fantasy world of C.S. Lewis' Narnia through a wooden wardrobe within which lies a mirror, reflecting back the fantasy of childhood into the dull adult world, and through it enter the wintry woods of Narnia. In Shakespeare's Midsummer Night's Dream the forest manifests fairies and conceals Titania and King Oberon. Childhood, with its illusions and fantasies, is just a stage in life, but it is a story we can get stuck in unless we keep growing. Adulthood arrives not so much by courtesy of age, but through seasons of getting lost, confused, tricked and defeated. We have to get lost to find our way.

Looking on from the forest margins are four mature oaks. I dash over to stand next to one for shelter, its finger-like branches offering an umbrella from the baptism of rain. Its trunk is rough on my cold hands as I measure it. Eighteen hands around. Thousands of immature acorns adorn the base, cracking beneath my feet, as I circle the tree, hand to hand. Here feels safe, for now. I get my breath back then dart into open space, the rain like a sail, a thick opaque screen I have to somehow penetrate. More oaks thrust up from the earth like defiant fists groping at the sky, branches rinsing themselves in the downpour. I must keep running. I don't know why, or where to, or for whom, but a primal voice in my gut urges me on: *Just keep going*.

Thirty minutes later, skin saturated beneath my running kit, I stop beneath a silver birch which has been struck by lightning. The forest floor is littered with shining white branches scattered like fallen swords, the result of 60 mile an hour winds the day before I arrived. A voice from behind a hawthorn thicket makes me spin round and I see a lady in a black dress approaching. "Have you seen a donkey?" she shouts. Black mascara runs in forked lines down her face, like lightning. "My donkey seems to have got loose and made a run for it" she shouts above the crushing rain. "Have you seen it? Have you seen a donkey? It's come loose" she says, as if repetition were an incantation to woo the lost animal back to her. "There's lots of ponies in open land half a mile away" I shout, pointing with a stabbing finger, "but I didn't see a donkey". I look along the the line of my finger, then turn back but she has disappeared through the hawthorn like an apparition. For the next hour I find myself looking for a wayward ass in torrential rain, alone, wondering what I will do with it if I find it. Or perhaps I am the lost ass.

This is no tame place. Our words "wood" and "wildness" share the same root word, *wald*. So much runs free here, like a wandering mind, uprooting and re-routing itself. Just when I think I am lost again, I spot the four oaks, the forest guardians, unmoved, branches nodding as if to say "we told you so".

I recall another dream from when life was at its most uprooted: I was on a theatrical stage, parading in a woman's dress, wearing a purple wig, my face covered in thick make-up. I froze on stage and tried to rip my wig off but couldn't, so I jumped off stage, walking boldly into the audience asking for a mirror so I could see myself. Others on stage rushed after me, wrestling each mirror away from my grasp, as if the cast were in on some secret that I must not look in the mirror. I snatched a glimpse in a handheld mirror: I looked like a clown. Shocked, I smeared the lip-stick across my face with the back of my hand, like streaks of blood. The actors around me (people I knew in the real world) became livid, chasing me out the theatre, the clown's wig dangling, its artificial curls knocking against my back as I sprinted, screaming in search of a safe place.

We shouldn't be surprised when the content of our life circumstances overflows into nighttime thoughts as a non-conscious attempt to make sense of things. Lost bearings trigger all kinds of emotion, especially confusion, a small but powerful and often disregarded ingredient in the onset of anxiety. We prefer to avoid confusion because it threatens our sense of knowing things. "For sure, certainly, absolutely" we prefer to say. Then we know where we are. Psychologists say people are more anxious about uncertainty than they are about certain pain. Confusion is like a compass needle in the brain spinning in search of a new direction. The word comes from the Latin *confundere*, meaning to mingle together. Confusion is not something from which to back off, because it can actually be a unifying emotion, mingling old ideas with new, fusing what was previously understood with new knowledge. Confusion is a necessary step before new insight. Confusion leads us into liminal mental space and forces us to ask new questions. It can become, if we embrace it, a creative energy opening up larger possibilities. Rather than "I don't know" and shutting down because we feel under threat, we can begin with "I don't know...yet" and "I wonder if..." and "What I'm curious about is..." We need curiosity to navigate life.

The rain withdraws but oak, beech, birch continue weeping drops, from leaf to lower leaf, like an heirloom handed down between generations. Everything returns to unspoken agreements of stillness, until a procession of a dozen wild cattle crackle through fern like breaking radio silence. Standing aside, I watch them pass in mournful parade, their skins slick with rain, then spin as a single black beast with a white face stalks me from behind. A thin stream lies between us, plus an old car tyre hanging from an oaken branch, swaying like a hypnotist's pendulum. Who will fall under the spell? The bull steps into the stream with a laser beam gaze on me. My heart races. I am confident it can't use a tyre swing, Tarzan-like, to reach me, but for precaution I climb a half-fallen oak choking in holly, feet sliding on the moss as I ascend. Once I am several metres off the ground I attempt to blend in with a trunk half the width of my body, which is difficult in a fluorescent orange jacket. The bull stares, before finally rejoining the slow procession of its peers. I leap to the floor causing a crick-crack of twigs.

My phone indicates "No Service". I have no idea where I am. Forests are full of shadows and hiding places, spaces to wander and encounter the unfamiliar. Yet they also pulse with patience. Forests are not in a rush. Perhaps this is why writers throughout time have used them as stages not only for psychological change where children lose their way into adulthood, but the slow pace of spiritual transformation too. "We breathe with trees" said Thomas Merton, the American Trappist monk. Trees are mentioned on the first page of Genesis in the Bible, in the first Psalm, the first page of the New Testament and the first page of Revelation. Jesus Christ died on a rootless, branchless tree. Both Hindus and Buddhists revere trees as intrinsically sacred and Prince Siddhartha Gautama experienced enlightenment while sat beneath the heart-shaped leaves of the bodhi fig tree, becoming a Buddha, or "Awakened One". But the forest is more than trees: it homes thousands of insect species, birds, mammals, lichen, fungi, plants, and wild ponies scavenging for porridge. The forest is a matrix, life nested within more life, branching up and out, hyphae penetrating down, an inter-connected society both above and below. They give more than they take. They hold wisdom I do not have. It is difficult to feel self-important in them.

There is a striking similarity in look between a forest root system, with its overlapping root-branches, and the neural map of the human brain. Dendrites, the structures on the neuron that receive electrical messages in the brain, comes from the Greek *dendron* meaning tree. The brain is not organised like a to-do list. The brain's neural map mirrors the knuckled finger-fans found across and beneath the forest floor. No wonder we find it hard to "think straight" sometimes when the brain itself is a forest-like network.

Everything here finds itself in oscillation: Torrential rain shifts to burning sun. Sun-blotches and dark shadows interplay. Malty coniferous pine blends with musty oak. Open heathlands where ankles are scratched by gorse become soothed by heather. Sight is whisked up into the canopy but is then thrust down into the undergrowth. Silence holds until wild ponies and deer crash through. Old arguments resurface in the mind before a new insight drops like a blink of sunlight. I find myself constantly going in and coming out, lost then found, on the brink of anxiety before serenity returns. I am an outsider, an imposter, yet also feel at home in something larger and older than myself.

Roger Deakin knew trees better than many, completing the manuscript for his final book "Wildwood: A Journey Through Trees" just before his tragic death in summer of 2006 from a brain tumour. "When I pleach the ash tree" said Deakin, "I have to wound it, and the tree fights back from the wound and forms a callous to heal itself." The process continues, cells dividing, until the wound becomes the unifying point between two trees. "The cambium of one tree begins to grow into another, until the trees are no longer separate organisms but a single being with shared sap and circulation" wrote Deakin. I find this breath-taking, the tree-wound transforming itself into a magnificent reconciliation. Mingling old and new, a redeemed confusion. "There are no longer eight separate trees" said Deakin, "but a single one". I sense his delight. The forest confuses, confounds, humiliates, penetrates, yet has a healing effect. We enter them pleached, but leave them unified.

By chance rather than choice, I meet the winding B3056 as the sun appears, and within a few minutes am running through the village of Beaulieu, founded in the 13th century and whose name, from the French, means "Beautiful Place". The village is celebrated for its classic cars, home to the National Motor Museum founded by the last Lord Montagu. A collection of classic cars rest idle at the roadside. A sporty red one, roofless in the sun but with dripping wet interior, displays a sign printed on A4 paper sellotaped in a higgeldy-piggeldy fashion on its smeared windscreen. "Hire Me" it says, in Arial typeface. I reach the Beaulieu River mill pond beside Palace House, formerly home to Lord Montagu who in the 1950s when opening the house and gardens to the public for the first time greeted them with five veteran cars in his entrance hall. A novel twist on overflow parking. I sit by the river, beneath a diseased horse chestnut tree planted to commemorate 50 years of the Beaulieu estate. I stop the clock on my phone so time stands still: I have 2 hours 59 minutes 59 seconds left to run. Eating an apple beneath the tree I wait for enlightenment, which doesn't arrive.

I must keep going before lactate acid wrecks my ability to move. From the village I follow the B-road, running through open heathland, stroking bracken feathers as I pass, watching holly blue butterflies flirt with cabbage whites, and gold finches yo-yoing between thickets, playing chase. The land is a dozen shades of green, except for... Aaaargh! The rage resumes, triggered by the sight of a plastic milkshake cup gleaming white at the roadside, a curvy M on its side. I stare at the cup, the plastic lid, the plastic straw. The object triggers a chain reaction and I feel, actually not just anger, but sheer sadness. I curse the air. I curse how Big Business can be so small-minded and short-sighted, my futile judgements falling between gorse spikes, lost forever. For the next mile I argue with myself about whether I should have picked the litter up. *But it's not my litter*, my brain argues, *I can't tidy up the whole world*. Then a different voice. *Nobody's expecting you to save the whole world, but you can do this one thing.* I run a mile back, in defeat or hope I don't know, pick up the soggy milkshake cup and stuff it into the backpack. More weight, more damn weight.

In his 1978 documentary "On The Edge of the Forest", economist E.F. Schumacher stands amongst Australian eucalyptus, talking in a state of awe. "The forest is hundreds of years old. The waterfall? Eternal" he says, "but we have become so accustomed to thinking that two, three years is a long time. We think in such short time spans" says Schumacher. His book "Small is Beautiful" was the first book I read after finishing university, a refreshing contrast to years of studying accountancy and law books. Written in 1973 amidst an energy crisis and the emergence of globalisation, Schumacher's philosophy struck me as both sensible and sustainable. "If we don't live more simply then it will be forced on us by the facts of the universe" he said. "Maximise satisfaction, minimise consumption" was his mantra.

"We don't know what we are doing" he says "when we remove one element from the forest". Health depends not on being free of blemish, but having a balanced system, each part feeding other parts. "Even dead wood plays a part", he says, "the tidy human mind says it should be removed...it may look dead but it is full of life, mosses, little flowers, insects, worms". Life regenerates itself, but if we become "too violent, too cocksure, too selfish" he warns, we will destroy our existence. We enter the forest, and the forest enters us. We co-exist.

Reaching Stockley enclosure I realise the tent, pitched at Roundhill, is only a mile away. I resisted the ice cream van at Hatchet Pond and a cold pint at Monty's Inn in Beaulieu but I won't resist the tent. With my knee strapped and aching from Snowdon, I need rest. My marathon, my rules. I crouch down like a feeding pony, scamper in, lie down and fall asleep. An hour later I exit the tent by crawling. The sun strikes my face and last night's dream about my father and the cardboard boxes becomes clearer. The forest dendrites seem to be working upon my unconscious mind. The meaning of the dream, I think, is to put away old ideas I had about masculinity (three men breaking down the boxes together), and something about going to a higher level to reclaim what it is to be a father (climbing the hill to erect a memorial). The meaning needs to percolate.

The phone timer says 2 hours 10 minutes still to run. I re-enter the forest in late afternoon. The sun has burned away the clouds. I push between low-lying conifer pine branches, like turnstile barriers, weaving a way amongst dense coniferous plantation and reach the forest's darkest part where pines are speared into the ground, blade-tips aimed at the sky. Pine cones crack underfoot. There is destruction everywhere. *"The tidy human mind..."* No, this isn't destruction, it is life in the process of slow regeneration. Ducking beneath fallen trunks, I clamber over recently felled mature trees, jagged branches clawing at my jacket. The soundscape is different here, muted. A fallow deer bursts away, its white hind shrinking from view. "Nature transmits something" says author Eckhart Tolle, "when we contemplate nature, we take on its qualities". I stand, motionless as oak. "Just...slow...down" said Therapist John. Between the mewing of a buzzard there is a deep, sober silence here I want to absorb. I slow my own breathing but still feel out of sync, still too fast, breathing in a different timezone. This forest has accumulated slowness over hundreds of years, its lungs reaching deeper inside the body of the earth

I remain still, breathing with the trees.

There is a movement in the thicket. A pig? A goat? I feel alert, in case it is something which doesn't approve of the fluorescent orange thing trespassing through its home. I stand still as my heart drums. Then my eyes meet with those of a female sika deer, white-spots on its red-brown coat, a bambi-lookalike.

Clambering out the forest, I cross Balmer Lawn, a 500 acre lowland grazing plain, notable for thousands of humps which look like giant bubble wrap. A man in a tracksuit meditates beneath an oak, although he could be dead and propped up for show. It's difficult running over the bumps so I re-enter the forest. The sinking sun illuminates all that is twisted and broken on the forest floor including two fungi, side by side, like father and son. I circle and twist through trees, legs aching but enjoying the dance, running spirals, loops and laps for more than an hour. Nothing is linear, yet all is pattern. I have felt so lost these last few years but the loss helps me remember to play, without goal or ambition, a permission to be rather than a pressure to perform. With 20 minutes left on the timer, I spot a pub in the village of Brockenhurst. A pint of Snakecatcher has been well earned. Sitting on a bench in the pub yard, I notice peculiar graphics on the pint glass: a flatbed truck, deck chairs, a signpost, and the word Slowdownland. Slow Down Land. Ha! Two men wearing splattered white dungarees on the next bench stare at me, looking puzzled, as I hold the pint glass right next to my eye and stare into it, sunlight filling the empty vessel.

Each return step toward the tent hurts. It was ridiculous expecting to go from zero back to 26.2 miles (or a five hour run) in just a few weeks. Shadows extend along the grit track past Balmer Lawn and dusk arrives as I reach the lane which takes me to the campsite. Then it happens. Hooves clatter the road in urgency, like an impending storm. Three, four....no, seven wild ponies gallop, I assume chasing me. I attempt a hobbled sprint, fear rising in my throat, before the relief as the first pony overtakes, then two others passing on either side, ignoring me in their joyful shenanigans. It is a noisy home-coming.

I lie in the tent. It is cold. Tomorrow's forecast is torrential rain all day. "I went to the woods because I wished to live deliberately" wrote Thoreau. But I came to the woods to wander, to get lost and slow down. I roll over in the sleeping bag and hear thunder, not from the sky but the ground. Wild ponies are restless in the dark, their hooves shuddering the earth, drumming past the tent. I imagine a lost donkey racing with them. The woods have worked a spell upon me.

AUTUMN

> "Your willingness to look at your darkness is what empowers you to change"
>
> —Iyanla Vanzant

My first day volunteering in the local forest is spent breaking necks of ferns. Four of us gather in a barn with a leaky roof. Half the barn is occupied by a shiny tractor. A trestle table, swamped with tea bags, mugs and jars, trembles as two kettles boil at the snail pace of the generator. Paul, the guy with bright eyes giving out instructions, explains our tasks for the day using a pencil sketch of the forest, alerting us to the presence of stag beetle piles and where new heather is coming through from the rare acid heathland. If I just yank the ferns out of the ground, Paul tells me, this will reinforce their "subterranean energy system", but by breaking their necks the ferns' energy will be wasted and therefore weaker next year. This will reduce competition with the rare heather and gorse, whose small summertime flowers provide pollen for butterflies and bees. Save for the rapid "tseep-tseep" soundtrack of dunnocks, we work in sunlit silence, although for a few strange minutes rain falls from a blue sky. I find gun cartridges, evidence of deer poaching, and learn how to saw 'gob cuts' into mature pine trees to help them fall in a chosen direction, allowing more light and space for the heather and gorse to thrive.

The Heart of England Forest, where we are working, builds on the vision of maverick publisher Felix Dennis who bought the land in 1995. The forest survives within a footprint of ancient woodland and its resurrection is still in its infancy. The forest presently stretches from Sheriffs Lench in south Worcestershire to Honeybourne in Warwickshire, reaching up to Studley. The two millionth tree was planted here in 2022. The reuniting of these patches of forest - the Royal Forest of Feckenham and Forest of Arden - is a task beyond a lifetime, but the intention is to create a mosaic of habitats, woven between meadows and farmland. A slow yet deliberate work of reconciling parts into a whole. Working within it as a volunteer becomes part of my "geography of hope", a place to think, work, learn and rejuvenate.

Research by the University of Exeter shows that two hours a week immersed in nature is good for body and mind: it reduces joint pain and blood sugar levels, strengthens the heart, arm and leg muscles, and lowers symptoms of depression and anxiety. This should come as no surprise, yet when we face pressure and stress, for many of us it is easier to drift towards unhealthier ways of coping than to step outdoors, fill our lungs with air and get our hands dirty. I arrive home from my first day volunteering, fingers tingling with dozens of tiny punctures from clearing brambles, but feeling renewed.

A few weeks later, I return. From the shed we collect saws of different sizes including the "slashers" as Paul calls them, plus a first aid kit bag large enough to fit a child in. We walk past the stag beetle stack, the sun rising to the top of the pines. Baby buzzards squeal, their cry piercing the otherwise quiet mesh of wood and wildlife. There is an adult buzzard stationed halfway down the spear-trunk of a pine, its feathered body the same colour as the tree. It panics its wings so it appears as if the tree has come to life and is waving at us. We slash brambles and bracken to clear an old ride (path), allowing more light to reach the forest floor. We saw through fallen pines, placing logs into untidy stacks where they can rot to their hearts content. Rolling a rotting trunk out of the way reveals an ant nest and a toad. A vole scurries across the sunlit ride. I see more wildlife in one morning than I normally do in a year.

Slash, sweat, saw, stack. Simple work, crafting gaps for more light to come. "The last task" announces Paul, sweeping his forearm across his brow, "is to shift that!", pointing to a twelve foot long wood and metal frame. "It's the high shooting seat the pheasant shooters dumped ages back." The shooting seat is more cumbersome than heavy. We disentangle the seat from brambles and nettles, then walk a quarter of a mile together through the forest carrying it on our shoulders like coffin-bearers, before placing it by the shed. "I'll think about how we can re-use it" says Paul, "because everything has another life."

"We still need to coppice more hazel near the bean field" explains Paul. "It's a bit premature but the August storms have caused damage. We can protect the new life from the deer by using the cut-off branches to make tee-pees over them, then tie the tee-pees at the top with brambles". His eyes dart between the four of us gathered near the open boot of his car, which he uses as his seat. At his feet is a bucket of acorns in which he plunges his right arm as if picking a raffle ticket. "If we can get this bucket full of acorns today that would be great too" he says, "as we're hoping to collect a hundred kilos of acorns before the squirrels and deer get to them."

As the others cut hazel staffs as thick as wrists down to ground level using them to construct a dead hedge, I wander off in search of acorns, Paul's bucket hooked over my arm like a shopping basket. At first I can't see any, then my eyes attune and I see them. First just as singles, then couples, then families of them, until the forest floor reveals itself as a universe of acorns, as if the acorns present themselves from the undergrowth, returning to the surface for air rather than having fallen from above. I crouch to collect them, scooping them in my hands, as if gathering fallen library books. I squat, then stoop, then become near-parallel with the earth, arms spreading like tree roots, a tee-pee of ferns covering my body. Dozens of spent gun cartridges litter the forest floor too. I collect cartridges, dropping them into the bucket: purple ones, yellow ones with rusted rims, blood-red ones, white ones with teasing splits up their side. Acorns mix and tumble in the bucket filling the empty plastic cartridges as if eager to be triggered to life. The bucket looks full of tiny green grenades, a time bomb of potentiality. The weight of a future forest sits in the bucket. "What I'll do" says Paul, as we walk to the shed, "is put the acorns in a massive pot of water. The healthy ones will sink to the bottom, and the diseased or nibbled ones will float to the top, because they have more air in them. I can filter out the diseased ones that way."

As I drive away, Paul doesn't see me waving to him. His gaze, and both *hands, are submerged in the bucket, searching for that winning ticket, or perhaps preparing to detonate the future. The next dot has been on pause since February but as the autumn equinox nears, it is time.*

DARTMOOR

In solitude we no longer escape ourselves

Watching from a pop-up tent on Holwell Down the sun seems as close as a heat-seeking missile, an amber disk descending behind Top Tor. It sinks lower, until **O** becomes **Ọ** as if perching on the edge of a cliff. The sky is afire, then darkness. The autumn equinox is a matter of days away, sun and moon on an invisible see-saw. I pivot from the sunset to watch the moon rise, a gold coin against a lilac cloth, ascending between Hound Tor and Black Hill.

Fifteen runners are camping here, more will arrive tomorrow for race day, with distances of between 6 miles and a 31 mile ultra marathon available. My camping neighbours are, according to the van registration plate, from Slovenia. From the open boot of their souped up camper van they assemble a makeshift shower causing waste water to puddle on the grass reflecting the moonlight. The van accommodates three beds although from the intimate noises during the night I'm not sure they ever reach their own duvets. I lay on my back, half in, half out of the tent, staring at stars, each vibrant and singular. The moor feels like a lung, expanding, inhaling the night.

Due to the altitude of the moor, when I unzip the tent just after 6 a.m. instead of a glorious sunrise there is only mist moving like thievery, a pale finger of light poking through. I put a woolly hat on and shuffle lower into the sleeping bag, stealing whatever rest I can before race preparations begin. Whereas a fen like Wicken is a lowland, watered from beneath by underground springs, a moor is an upland, saturated by rain. Like its nearby neighbour, Bodmin Moor, Dartmoor is a duvet of marsh, laying upon an acidic peat mattress, contained in a granite frame.

With runners gathered in the marquee for the race briefing, we are warned about how many course route signs have been removed overnight by local farmers. Race officials are out in the sunrise-mist replacing whatever signs they can. "Look out for these orange arrows" the race director says, waving an example, "and also the red and white tape tied to tree branches" (which gets removed after the race). Thirty-nine of us move across the field toward the inflatable start line for the marathon. Nearly everyone carries a back-pack and the usual running clutter. Carbohydrate gels, bottles, tubes and whistles stick out from waistbands, shoulders and heads, like loose wiring. Race flags flinch in the breeze, and behind the flags the granite bulge of Haytor Rocks sits Buddha-like, a detached observer.

My left knee is heavily strapped, still tender from falling on Snowdon, not helped by then running 27 miles in the New Forest. My objective is to just start and reach one checkpoint at a time. A countdown is yelled through the mist. "Ten, nine, eight..." I exhale. Race number pinned on? Yes. Straps tight? Yes. "Two, one... off you go!" As runners flee across the start line, because I no longer have a watch which works, I stop to ask the race director the cut off time for today. "The course shuts at 5.30pm" he says. That means up to nine hours of trail hobbling.

Dartmoor National Park was once part of the royal forest, but is now a largely treeless landscape, stripped bare over centuries by mesolithic hunters, tin miners and iron smelters, one generation after another delving for reward beneath Dartmoor's skin. It has been grazed by sheep and ploughed with ponies from as far back as the twelfth century, leaving narrow strip fields called lynchets, a reminder of times when the climate here was drier and hotter and cereal crops were grown. Dartmoor is a place where much has been buried and much still remains a mystery. In the cave shelters at Buckfastleigh remains of interglacial animals such as hyena and rhinoceros have been found. The 76 granite stone rows and avenues that mark parts of the Dartmoor boundary suggest a landscape rich in prehistoric ritual from a time when the prevailing worldview didn't separate land and sky. Dartmoor is now a rare, final frontier of wildness. "You feel you're in a different time as well as place" says author William Atkins, describing Dartmoor as a place of "unreachable loneliness" where you go to hide. Twelve miles from today's start line, located in the centre of Dartmoor like an eye looking outward, is a category C men's prison, HMP Dartmoor in Princetown. Resting on the moor's south-eastern perimeter, like an eye looking inward is the 11th century Benedictine Buckfast Abbey.

Two solitudes: one enforced, the other invited.

Our first ascent leads to Smallacombe Rocks by which time I am at the back of the pack, accompanied by two ladies who are the official tail runners, there to make sure nobody gets left behind. I stop and stroke the granite rock and study lichen flake patterns. The ladies look concerned by my rock molestation but it is one thing to see the landscape from afar and quite another to feel its texture and temperature on your fingertips. I may never come this way again. The head says "rush", but the body says "notice". The descent takes us through knee-high bracken which smothers vast stretches of the moor, preventing regeneration of woodland, then a leap across a wide stream before weaving through woodland knotted with rowan and holly. I have to crouch and twist as if in tango with the wood. The route ascends again, up to the stone-stacked cairns at Black Hill, before a gradual descent to the first checkpoint on a single track lane near Ullacombe Farm.

Runners have been told to bring their own reusable bottles so there are no plastic cups, just inch-long slices of banana, watermelon triangles, pieces of dark chocolate, bowls of sweets and nuts. I scoop a handful of salted peanuts for the sodium before the sun sweats it all out, and refill a bottle with isotonic water. Keeping electrolytes in balance (such as sodium, potassium and calcium) is important as they not only control the flow of water in the body's cells, but are essential for heart, lung and brain function.

Today I want to experience solitude-on-the-move. There are many benefits to running alone: Having not showered for two days, I don't need to worry about hygiene, and I can dictate my own pace and style, stopping when and where I want. Another benefit is learning to be your own best encourager. It's just You vs. You out there. I leave a group of chatty runners crunching chocolate chunks at the checkpoint and venture on alone.

Solitude is being erased from our lives. It seems harder to get away from screens, machines, notifications and incessant technological noise. A recent study said half of us sleep with phones in our beds (under the pillow perhaps?), like digital teddy bears. For those of us caught in the machinations of work, we are pulled and pushed in a chaotic swell of demands and deadlines, time pressures and targets. We drown in crowds. The paradox of volume is that the louder we become the less anyone *really* listens. Noise, nausea, noxious. No thanks.

The gaps between people have shrunk, boundaries erased. "We meet at very short intervals" wrote Thoreau, hoeing his bean fields by Walden pond, "not having had time to acquire any new value for each other." No wonder we sometimes feel lop-sided: all crowd, no space. Social media thrives on this gapless culture: like, share, repost, link, favourite - each notification releasing a dopamine dollop in the brain triggering the pleasure and reward system. Our attention is their currency. "Look at this! Look at THIS!" Author Michael Harris describes our connection with massive social networks as a "phantom umbilical cord".

Solitude is presence more than absence, an active rather than passive process. Regathering at our core is not selfish, any more than it would be selfish to quench your thirst or clean your teeth. Self-centring sharpens our sensory attention from which others benefit. The world needs our true presence. It needs us fully Here, not half-in-half-out, so we can stand for what's true and leave a signature which lasts.

How can we actively protect ourselves from pondering those relentless questions that most humans seem to have: "*Am I enough? Good enough? Doing enough? Do I have enough? Am I liked enough?*" A useless narrative generated by a sense of deficit. Self-esteem has become dictated by the quantity of digital thumbs up, stars, hearts, kudos, ticks. "Seeking validation outside of yourself" says performance coach and author Brad Stulberg "is like salt water, it just leaves you thirsty for more." The internet cannot provide solitude, presence or peace of mind. Choosing to go off the map from time to time therefore becomes an act of rebellion and rebirth.

Solstice, from Latin, means "the sun comes to a stop". As the course rounds Yarner Wood on the moor's eastern side, I wonder about the practice of human solstice, of *Self-Stopping*, a chance to get our bearings about where we are, how we are and what's going on within us. Solitude involves both subtraction and addition. Occasionally subtracting ourselves physically, mentally and socially from crowds, screens and input from others gives us a chance to hear ourselves think and breathing space to see ourselves more realistically. As ancient Greek philosopher Plotinus wrote, we journey from the "alone" through the crowd into the "ALONE". But time on our own is not a one-way trip of disconnecting from the external world. The image of a monk contemplating in a cave is not something most of us are going to identify with. Being in one's own company for too long can breed unhealthy rumination where we get trapped in thought-circuits of our own making.

I had a friend who admitted, over a pint together, to feeling lonely. I asked him several times, "How are you, really? What are you feeling?" But he could only talk about abstract problems of philosophy and throw super-long words at me as a final line of defence. His intelligence became a form of stupidity. Stuck in his own mental loft, he was disconnected from his own visceral experience and sensation. He could think, but not feel. Impress, but not connect.

If at the end of a time of solitude you feel depleted rather than replenished, that's likely to be an indicator of too much rumination, those subtle negative "what if" patterns of thinking which pull you down. Solitude rarely leads to excitement, that is not its function, but we can feel re-attuned to ourselves and as a result become more attentive to others. The myth is that solitude only applies to introverts. We are wired differently to one another and have different needs and expectations when it comes to relationships, but solitude is something only we can do for ourselves, however much you need and however frequently you need it. Nobody else can do solitude for you. Having taken a mental deep breath we must then return to those around us.

As a fierce sun burns away the mist, I am grateful for the cover of Houndtor Wood. Beech and birch leaf-tips appear dipped in gold. Ploughing through chest-high bracken I spot a solitary fly agaric toadstool at my feet, six inches wide, distinctive with its fairytale red flat-cap, dotted with white spores like something from The Smurfs cartoons. Lowering to its level, it looks like a capital **T** and is the first I have seen in my adult life. For some reason I feel protective toward it. Fly agaric, also known as fly amanita, has psychoactive and hallucinogenic properties having been used in a sacred drink in India and Iran for thousands of years. Like many fungus, it has a companionable relationship with a specific land plant, in this case birch trees. I later learn this is known as a "mycorrhizal" relationship. (For weeks "mycorrhiza" became my new favourite word although chances to use it in conversation were limited). Birch supplies the fungus with carbon needed to make its hairlike threads, called hyphae, which are even thinner than the roots. In exchange, the fungus supplies the birch with nutrients, such as phosphorus and nitrogen. The well-being of each is improved by the other. The fungus looks solitary yet plays its part in a complex process of give and take. This becomes my favourite metaphor for the relationship between solitude and the wider world.

Without exposing our senses to the expansive space of moors, seas and mountains, we become short-sighted, forever enclosed in constructs: houses, cars, shops, offices. The openness of the moor is an invitation to escape the boxed-in, on-screen version of life. Open landscapes open minds. Like the fungi and the birch, there is a mycorrhizal relationship between our well-being and the environments we inhabit.

The race route follows the River Bovey through Woodash where the path becomes uneven, hundreds of football-sized boulders making it impossible to run. I stub toes, go over on an ankle, slip and stumble, despite moving slowly. Rowans tower overhead, their leaves appearing like hiking boot footprints silhouetted against the sky. A steep narrow path is overshadowed by deciduous canopy creating the sense of hiding in an envelope waiting to be withdrawn. I reach Old Clam Bridge where a sign warns "Use at your own risk". It is clear why: the bridge is a rivened, rotten tree trunk laid across a stream at an angle that makes balance upon it impossible. *Is this really the way?* I spot red and white tape dangling from a rowan tree further along the path which leads to another wooden signpost pointing towards Lustleigh Cleave. With a third of the marathon complete, I arrive alone in the hamlet of Manaton where the second checkpoint offers watermelon and brown banana leftovers. It has taken two and half hours to complete just 10 miles, a reflection of how challenging the terrain has been and how distracted by toadstools and lichen-covered rocks I have become.

Squeezing through a gap in a wall by St. Winifred church, a building dressed in granite and volcanic stone, the church clock begins sounding eleven chimes. The layered canopy of beach and oak softens the church bell-sound, so the woods become a sonorous bowl. It is like running through music. I gaze upward into the space, inhaling late-summer colours, textures, scents. The bell-chimes remind me of Perotin's "Beata Viscara", a solitary voice filling a cathedral infiltrating every quanta of space. *I am here. This is it.* A living quietness moves through everything.

A runner in an adjacent field is going in the wrong direction, perhaps looking for a lost donkey or an early way out. "Hey mate! It's this way!" I shout. He finds a way back to the path and I point to the signs to convince him. "I was too busy talking to myself" he laughs, "I need to pay attention". Karol explains he is a keen triathlete, but wanted to try running trails, this being his first time. "You chose a challenging one to start with" I say. We are still talking when bracken and brambles rise to above head height, and I lose track of him. I wait for him at Luckdon Farm as the route changes direction, but there is no sign and I worry he is lost again, so continue alone westward along the base of Easdon Tor and past Whooping Rock, named because of the sound the wind makes as it passes through the rocks.

An orange arrow stapled to a stile indicates a sharp turn through a field. Climbing over it, I see another runner who has missed the turn, running up a hill in the wrong direction. I shout out four times before he stops and returns downhill. "Who knows where I would have ended up!" he jokes, then follows me over the stile past Torhill Farm. After stopping to pick wild blackberries, I catch up with him expecting to talk for a while, but as we cross Hayne Brook and begin the climb together onto moorland he turns towards me abruptly, "Dude, just run ahead and leave me alone". During the day, I noticed more than a dozen men walking alone along the moor, none offering more than a glance or nod, each radiating a "leave me alone" vibe. This is fair enough, they are not hiking across the moor to socialise. "When the eye finds nothing to fix itself on" says author William Atkins describing English moors, "the mind turns inwards".

When I first camped on Tenby beach and had nothing to do other than cope with 90 hours of solitude, even the task list seemed a never ending distraction:

collect firewood
rearrange firewood
swim in sea
shake sand off towel
boil water for tea or cook soup
re-stack stones around fireplace
re-position rocks holding the tent pegs down
stare at horizon
think thoughts
write in journal
walk along beach
nap
collect more firewood (return to top of list)

Each year, upon arrival, I would collect rocks from the shoreline and create a large circle of them in the sand, before pitching my tent in the middle of the circle. Without knowing why, I would walk the circle, three times anti-clockwise, asking for protection. In a way, I found comfort in the ritual. A self-imposed certainty during a time of great uncertainty. A connection to something ancient or just a chance to be weird. The first year I didn't do the ritual and an electrical storm struck in the night. The tent succumbed to storm violence leaving my body shrink-wrapped in the sodden tent fabric and collapsed poles, as if enclosed in a chrysalis. It was terrifying, lying there in the destroyed tent, in total darkness, in the storm, alone for four hours.

Each year on the beach, hours would pass before remembering there was nothing to achieve. I was there to get precisely nowhere. That was the Point: a self-chosen detox from Progress. Sometimes solitude is posited as a glorious spiritual state of being, but in solitude, we can no longer escape ourselves. It can be boring and irritating, dealing with the endless distractions of the mind. Solitude is no guarantee for clarity, but it increases the chances of listening to yourself, revealing the occupying and competing voices of the personality. Self-talk doesn't usually sound as angelic as "Beata Viscara" filling a cathedral. Thoughts can be relentless, compulsive and argumentative. Brains are noisy buggers.

Solitude is a healthy companion to other things like friendships, regular time outdoors, talking therapy, learning something new, gratitude, decent rest. Everyone's "personal mycorrhiza" is going to be different, but it is solitude, rather than loneliness, isolation or aloofness, that we need to recover. In solitude we start to distinguish between our own voice and that of the masses, the unthinking crowd who follow the prevailing media narratives of the day without critical reflection. Solitude forces us to stop fitting in. Truth becomes clearer. We discover what we stand for.

When camping on Tenby beach, repeating the visit each year for five years, I noticed the constant, inevitable current of loss that flows beneath and within daily life: another minute, hour, day, month, year gone. In solitude we confront the underlying sadness that our individual life is temporary. This is hard, and possibly why we do everything to avoid it and stay busy. Nearly everything within us resists the fact that one day we die. But acknowledging the reality of finitude allows something else to arise in its place, something with the texture of acceptance, a fresh inclination for what's happening now. This is it. Just this.

A tent on a beach pitched within a circle of rocks, with a fallen tree trunk beside it, attracted passers-by. Usually men. Whereas dogs would lift their leg and piss on my fire without permission, their owners would stop and talk. "Been here long?" they often asked. "I'd love to do that someday" many said, pointing at the tent, the rocks, the nest of driftwood by the fire. Each year during the few days I was there, at different times, men asked to sit on the "tree bench" and we would stare at the sea together, often saying nothing for twenty minutes. Just sitting together. "Thanks for that" they would say, before leaving. One told me about losing his parents in the same month and how his dog kept him going during hard times. Another told me why the world is doomed. A man in his eighties told me what it was like being a London taxi driver in the 1960s and coping with a business going bankrupt, throwing both his hands in the air like a magician who made something vanish. A man with one leg shorter than the other spoke of his wife's death from cancer earlier in the year. "I still don't know how to cook for myself" he said, his eyes straining toward the sea as if his wife might return from the horizon. The fallen tree became a Freudian couch. Each year as I prepared to leave the beach, I rearranged the charred rocks from the fireplace into a phrase, like "BE STILL" or "PAUSE". We don't really have the words to contain one another's suffering.

With Honeybag Tor towering to the left a runner joins me and tells me about being physically assaulted two years ago. "I didn't see it coming" he says, "the guy was drunk and punched me on the back of the head so I hit a wall, breaking every bone in my face, my eye socket, jaw, the lot. I was self employed but suddenly I couldn't see, which isn't helpful when your job is a graphic designer". I ask him about rehabilitation, amazed he is running today's half marathon. "I just started walking, gave myself a realistic goal" he says "I just wanted to get my life back". "I know it sounds odd" he continues, "but when you're out here" and he points at Honeybag Tor, "the greens are greener, the blues are bluer. Going through what I did made me think about what I really want to do. Look, here we are, out on a Saturday morning, doing THIS. I'm BACK!", raising his arms in triumph. At that moment a common lizard sprints across the dusty track in front of us, arresting our attention and causing us both to stop, before it disappears into undergrowth. We reach checkpoint three, wish each other well and part company, having different finish lines to pursue.

The Two Moors Way leads through the thick woodland of Heathercombe then across fields, bathed in sun. I run through a farm causing a dozen geese to flap in panic, and as the path becomes steep and my knees hurt I alternate walking and running. With King Tor rising to the south side, the view stretches not for miles, but for eons. I rush through checkpoint four at mile 18 where the volunteers are trying to keep the food shaded from the heat but the banana slices have become goo. I refill my bottle then keep moving, with the route turning southward past Hookney Tor. Black Welsh Mountain sheep and Cheviots, both hardy breeds, are scattered like pepper and salt across the hillside. I wave at a herd of alpacas and run past stacks of rudimentary beehives made of old milk crates and chest drawers, teetering precariously, bound in blue strapping.

I'm just enjoying myself when a flatbed truck speeds past, the driver with his shirt sleeves rolled up. He speeds back and forth half a dozen times, causing me to feel apprehensive. By the conifer forest of Soussons Down, he parks awkwardly, blocking the lane and standing in my way, hands on hips. "Oi, I've lost my cows" he says as I approach his truck. Whereas I am escaping the herd, today his herd have escaped him. "Sorry, I haven't got them" I hear myself say as if I might have his cows hidden under my t-shirt. Then we both look up because two aircraft have left a vapour trail creating the appearance of an X in the sky. We stare, each trying to decipher a meaning. "I don't think your cows are up there either" I say. He grunts, throws himself into the driver seat and speeds up the lane.

At the final checkpoint two young women gush with encouragement, offering all the cake anyone could ever eat. "You'll need it 'cos there's an incline next" one of them says, "then it goes down a bit, and then..." and they pause before saying in unison "there's the REALLY REALLY big hill at the end", both laughing in high-pitched tones.

Beyond a bracken-clad gulley the view suddenly expands in every direction. Two Tors crown the hilltops. I can see Bonehill Rocks where the finish line awaits, but first there is a steep descent into Widecombe in the Moor, a road so steep I have to run down backwards, a trick someone taught me when your knees are full of lactate acid and forward movement is too painful. I enter the village backwards, where a dozen people watch from their picnic blankets. Twenty-five miles run but there is no signage. Then a mother with young children calls out to me, "I think you're meant to go that-a-way" and points to a steep elevation lasting quarter of a mile. I pretend to pull my body up by an invisible rope, accompanied by grunting. Everything hurts but it's nearly done.

Finally, Bonehill Rocks. Half a mile over heathland, a final turn uphill to Holwell, a shimmy through a wooden gate and an attempt to sprint the last stretch to the finish line which protrudes from the horizon like a suitcase handle. It is the furthest I have run this calendar year (over 28 miles); and the steepest (total elevation of a mile); and the longest (7 hours and 11 minutes). I finish in the final handful of runners, more than two and half hours behind the winner. A dozen runners recline by the finish line, clustered like a Human Tor, applauding each finisher, congratulating one another on not getting lost.

The moorland sizzles in late afternoon sunlight. I stretch as many muscles as I can before collapsing in the tent, half-in, half-out. Solitude on the moor has settled my body, opened my heart, quietened my mind. "We simply need wild country available to us" wrote Wallace Stegner in "The Wilderness Letter", "even if we never do more than drive to its edge and look in. For it can be a means of reassuring ourselves of our sanity as creatures, a part of the geography of hope." Today was more than a run to the moorland edge to look in. It was a journey inward as well as a journey across. A long worthwhile effort enjoying solitude-on-the-go. I drive home that evening, aware that "one of the toughest races", as my Uncle Andrew used to describe it, is next. Another dot loitering on the edge of the map.

BEACHY HEAD

Gratitude is how we navigate life

Floorboards creak, giving away my dawn-time escape. Before leaving, I pick up the framed photograph in the hallway showing my Uncle Andrew approaching the finish line of the Paris marathon, the day he achieved his personal best time of 3 hours 44 minutes, fist raised in delight. The ability to raise his arm like that was one of the early things that motor neurone disease stole. I close the front door and wrench the handle upwards to lock it, just as Auntie Sandra instructed me to do over the bottle of wine we shared last night. I walk to the car past sleeping houses, disturbing puddles of orange lamplight on the pavement.

Along the A27 towards Eastbourne sycamore leaves slap the windscreen like high-fives. The car behind aggresses the rear bumper, attempting a piggy-back. I cut my speed until I am driving slower than the wind, just to infuriate them. The forecast is for heavy wind and rain. I don't want to run this marathon but perhaps something of my uncle's defiance lives on through this.

Author Claire Gillman, in her book about the power of liminal
ing to Love the Spaces In Between", says the difference
alk and a pilgrimage is the intention. Common to those
pilgrimages, she says, whether along established religious

routes such as the Santiago de Compostela in Spain or a self-devised journey, is an intention to "say please or thank you" on the journey. Only years later, looking back on the journey of these trail marathons can I recognise my own intention to say "thank you" to the people and places which have shaped my life, including my uncle.

Beachy Head marathon was my uncle's favourite race, completing it nine times. "One of the toughest" he used to say, with a total elevation gain of over 4300 feet. The place name "Beachy Head" has nothing to do with a beach but is most likely a corruption of the original French phrase "beau chef" in the early 18th century, meaning beautiful headland. Beachy Head itself is Britain's highest chalk sea cliff at 530 feet above sea level and holds the unenviable position of being the world's third most used place for attempting suicide, after San Francisco's Golden Gate Bridge and Japan's Aokigahara Woods. A Beachy Head Chaplaincy Team was set up in 2004 and patrols the area every day and evening, finding and preventing potential jumpers from going over the edge. They estimate they have responded to nearly 7,000 incidents, averaging more than one person every day.

It is a beautiful but sobering area in which to run, an interface between land and sea, between height and depth, between life lived and life lost. In the late seventeenth century local people attached lanterns to livestock grazing along the cliffside to trick sailors into thinking they were near other ships, rather than near land. A shipwreck provided local people with valuable produce and money. There was a local man, Jonathan Darby, the Parson of Friston and East Dean, whose job it was to bury the bodies washed up on the shore from shipwrecks. Rather than just bury the dead, he decided to intervene, attempting to save them from disaster. Parson Darby understood that a fixed point of reference was required, a light that would warn sailors how close they were to land, so he dug a series of holes in the cliff face ascending from the shore. On stormy nights he put lights on the ledges in the holes, often sitting alone in a cave during the night watching the sea. The work of Parson Darby was the provenance for what in 1834 became the 600-tonne granite Belle Tout Lighthouse, still standing today over 300 feet above the sea, just beyond Birling Gap. But even fixed things have to be moved sometimes. The cliffs here are 90 million years old but researchers at the University of Glasgow estimate that cliff erosion has increased 10-fold during the twentieth century and the deterioration is accelerating from more intense storms linked to changes in global temperature. The disappearance of a cliff is irreversible. The historic lighthouse nearly fell into the sea in 1998 and had to be slid on tracks 50 feet inland to save it (temporarily) from going over the edge.

The race marquee in Helen Garden on Eastbourne seafront swarms with over two thousand runners, many in fluorescent clothing. A man circles his arms like helicopter blades, limbering up, ready for take off. A woman in a pink tutu takes photographs of her friend. "Welcome-um to-to the Beachy-Chee Head-Head marathon-on" says the race announcer over the tannoy. "The cliff tops-ops are very exposed-osed so please keep away-way from the edge if you want to-to finish the race-ace". Along with advice about going to the toilet before the race we are reminded that checkpoints along route offer sausage rolls, soup and chocolate - additional incentives to stay away from the cliff edge. "And in today's race-ace there will be two runners-unners getting married-id during the race-ace". I hope these two people already know who they are. "They are members-bers of the Hundred Marathon-on Club-ub and by the end of the race-ace will be husband and wife-ife." As the crowd cheers I wonder if the groom will dare to put in a sprint finish in a display of premature acceleration.

The start line on Dukes Drive is a portal to the sky as there is an immediate 300 feet elevation gain, so the race begins at a crawling-clambering pace. Near the crest of the first hill a bagpipe player stands, his kilt flapping like a flag, melancholic music mixing with the wind. The course follows a chalk-ridge along the South Downs for around four miles, toward Willingdon Hill, brambles and hawthorn constantly snagging our elbows along the way. The soil type here is known as rendzina, suitable for slow growing plants such as yew, hawthorn and sweet briar, along with wildflowers with intriguing names: bastard toadflax, squinancywort and round-headed rampion.

At the first checkpoint whilst refilling my water bottle four nuns arrive with over-sized wooden crosses looped around their necks. "Sister Christine, will you stop fucking moaning and keep up" one of them says, offering a handful of jelly babies to Sister Christine who turns out to be a man.

We climb to Windover Hill, then a steep descent passing through the second checkpoint and Alfriston village, before another climb to the peak of Borstal Hill. The human-herd gallops ahead over rolling land and alongside edgeless flooded plains.

"Medic! Medic!" Hands wave, voices rise. A group of runners gather around a body lying in a chalk ditch. "MEDIC!" runners scream in frustration. I stop and turn with the intention of grabbing the medic who I passed moments ago who is oblivious to the emergency because the wind blows the screams for help in the opposite direction. Then the body moves. A man who looks like an experienced runner, face pinched with pain, clasps his right arm and stomach. The medic leads the injured man towards the ambulance parked at a nearby gate and the concerned gathering dissolves. Falling is easy along these high ridges and before the end of the race I count five bodies laying prostrate receiving medical attention as a result of a fall or exhaustion.

As we reach halfway, turning south toward Seaford and the coast, the wind bites at skin and all speech evaporates. The only sound I hear is the rippling of the paper race number safety-pinned to my top, clinging on for life. Running today is a protest against apathy, a raised finger to the gods. I imagine my uncle blaring his air horn "coming through" he would shout from the wheelchair, forging a way, although Beachy Head marathon wouldn't be ideal wheelchair racing territory.

If there was a quality my uncle exemplified I would say gratitude. A resolute attitude of thankfulness for family, the running community, the groups to which he belonged, the adventures he enjoyed. His gratitude barely wavered during the six years he lived with MND. What he taught me is that gratitude is a choice, a protective factor for the mind and heart. American Professor of Psychology, Martin Seligman, co-founder of the Positive Psychology movement, provides sound evidence of this. Decades of scientific research has led Seligman (who describes himself as a recovering melancholic) to conclude that it is vital we savour everyday sensory experience. Gratitude, Seligman suggests, must first be recognised before it can be felt. Deliberately noticing what is good, what is a relief, what is going well, is an important discipline. Acknowledging what you do have rather than what you don't. As a gateway into gratitude, instead of focusing on what appears to be the problem, ask yourself "what's *not* the problem?" Breathe these truths in, feel them in your fibres. Positive emotion isn't just subjective, it is biological, reducing blood pressure, lowering fibrinogen levels in the liver and improving cardiovascular health. Neuroscientists explain that gratitude stimulates two areas of the brain: the hypothalamus (which regulates stress), flooding the brain with the feel-good neurotransmitter dopamine, and the ventral tegmental area involved in the brain's reward system. Gratitude reduces stress as well as improving sleep quality, resilience and pro-social behaviour. Contemplation of the bigger picture keeps our own insecurities and needs the small size they usually are.

Gratitude has texture. Dr. Jeremy Sherman, writing in Psychology Today magazine, outlines different types of gratitude we might cultivate: gratitude for what is coming and gratitude for what is coming back; gratitude for what you have, gratitude for what you have already had and gratitude for what you are about to lose; there can be gratitude as gratuity (for a fair deal) and gratitude as platitude (for an opportunity). There can be gratitude for moments of sheer bliss. Even gratitude for feeling ingratitude is possible because it can motivate you to shift your focus. Gratitude is not something you force but something you allow. "There's a sort of awe at the core of it" says Sherman, "a humility you can't conjure up by yourself". You surrender to what is and gratitude comes, like spring water from a fountain. Gratitude becomes a principle, it is how we navigate our lives.

A poem I found earlier this week by Barbara Ras called "You can't have it all" closes with the line, "you can't have it all, but there is this". Running along the South Downs, battered by the winds and feeling deep fatigue, I quietly recite my own terrible version of the poem to keep a mindset of gratitude in tact:

You can't have it all, but there is the scuff of chalk.
You can't have it all, but it's not pissing down anymore.
You can't have it all, but there is this damn big open sky.
You can't have it all, but there will be hot cross buns at the next checkpoint.
You can't have it all…but there is this.

The table at checkpoint four at 16.7 miles has the promised hot cross buns, plus one-inch chunks of chocolate and squashed Danish pastries. Soup is poured from metal urns and an acoustic duo play, their amplifier volume at maximum, but I can't hear the music because of runners talking. Half-buried in a bush by the food table is a children's handmade poster, the words "Keep on going" drawn in bubble lettering. The child stopped colouring at the start of the word "going" as if the effort proved too much. It reminds me of the posters my daughter used to design to cheer me on at races. A child's enthusiasm can be so rejuvenating, with its belief in possibility. I hear my daughter's voice in my mind, "go on Daddy!" Now she's a runner, the fastest in the family, and was recently the fastest female in a local 10 km race but I don't think her speed is down to hot cross buns.

The race route continues through Friston Forest, past birch trees dropping yellow leaves like blobs of butter then leads to a staircase of over a hundred giant wooden steps, looking like something from Middle Earth. A leap over a stone wall at the top offers a long view looking out to Cuckmere Haven and the flooded lowlands. With my ankle hurting, instead of running down the hill I collapse into a ball and rolypoly all the way to the bottom, receiving a ripple of applause from a handful of spectators.

The punishing two and a half mile undulating stretch of the Seven Sisters Way along the cliff edge awaits, starting at Haven Brow and finishing with Went Hill at Birling Gap. It is torture for the knees and for the mind. Two years ago 50,000 tonnes of cliff collapsed and fell to the beach here. The following day a 23-year-old South Korean tourist jumped in the air for a photograph, slipped and fell to her death. I run as best as I can down each of the Seven Sisters hills, then walk up, too tired to think. It is relentless. I miss the St. John Ambulance checkpoint and just want to finish. Passing Brass Point, the sister hill in the middle of the seven, I pass a runner bent over, vomiting onto the grass. "I'm okay" she tells me when I check on her, "it's just a hangover". Facing into the wind, heads of runners retreat into their shoulders, as the grey skin of Belle Tout lighthouse appears ahead.

Sometimes effort becomes effortless, but not today. The run is hard, a steep slog, a dot on the map to claim. But then a 40 mile an hour wind pushes me up the final hill, another 300 feet elevation gain, brutal on the knees but I'm grateful for the wind assistance. The inflatable finish line anchored onto Dukes Drive nods with pride. I urge myself with the last atoms of strength I have toward it, grateful for what's coming up, grateful for what I'm leaving behind, grateful for mobility and poetry, hawthorns and hot cross buns. Grateful for all the ordinary moments of a life that when joined up together create the satisfaction of crossing a finish line. Perhaps gratitude IS the point, after all, a fixed point of light by which we navigate our lives. To feel contentment, wherever we place our feet.

Soaking in the bath at my Auntie Sandra's house, I anticipate the gratitude of turning another red dot on the map to blue. There are two weeks for these blisters to heal before the next marathon in South Wales, with a coastline even more demanding than the one today. Warm water rises to my chin, forming a beard of soap bubbles. Then I punch the air with a clenched fist, sending foam across the bathroom floor. Gratitude transcends lifetimes. I learned this from an uncle, smiling in Paris, raising his arm as if to say "count me in!"

The following day, driving home north on the M40, I wonder if there is another type of gratitude Dr. Sherman didn't mention in his list: gratitude for *gratitude*. Gratitude for the limitless capacity of gratitude, for its accumulative effect upon mind and heart, its ability to penetrate the core of human experience. Gratitude that no government can tax, prevent or control. Gratitude is a revolutionary choice, a heart-language that says "Yes!" to life in a world hell-bent on self-destruction.

A skein of geese honk overhead as I drive, temporarily cupped in the C of the new moon.

They fly in formation, the energy of their wings beating as one as their V-shape evolves to a W, like a two-pronged attack or just the revealing of symmetry. "Nearly home" I say, "nearly home".

GOWER PENINSULA

Remembering is an act of re-creation

Opening my eyes, reality is strewn across the hotel bedroom floor. All I see is a heap of muddy clothing. Two trainers are propped in the bath like drunkards against a wall, mud-slip marks tracing where they began the night before. My headache is either from running-induced dehydration or the quantity of beer consumed last night after the race. Beer for recovery purposes, of course. I forgot to stretch my legs after the race and the aching has begun. Aching for a time before all the pain and aching for a time in the future when all this becomes memory. Each limb feels turned inside out, strength discarded along yesterday's jagged coastline, drained by the sand dunes, the cairn-cluttered moorland, woodland trails, the rock climbing past limestone caves, the wooden-slatted paths along perilous cliff edges, the sapping mud bogs, and vast beaches.

The bedroom ceiling becomes a mental screen upon which remembered images project from the race: I remember the tangle of hazel trees through which I could see the inflatable finish line on Oxwich Bay beach, numerous white flags wrenching in the wind, where hundreds of human and animal footprints scattered this way and that amid the driftwood, cast like hieroglyphics.

But I remember most of all the rain flicking my face and the first sting of winter.

I stumble into the bathroom and chuck everything into the bath. Running tops, kit bag, face buff, gloves, jacket, leggings, compression socks, then step in with it, standing naked amid yesterday's filth. I turn the shower dial on. Nothing happens. How do you work the shower? I pull a string cord not sure if it is for the shower, the light or an emergency cord which will beckon a rescue party. All three would be welcome. Water dribbles from the shower head. I shiver and a thousand disjointed full stops form upon my arms and legs. I can smell bacon cooking downstairs.

More memories return. Before the beach finish line, I grasped a hazel tree to keep balance as I stumbled over tree roots knotted along the floor. There was a sign staked to the ground at ankle height with a large red number "1" indicating one mile to go. I saw a lone runner ahead, a shadow moving in the woodland. Why did it matter to overtake him? The act of remembering is like pulling up an anchor, each chain linked to another, moments revealing more moments. How far down, or back, does human memory go?

The shower bursts with freezing water and I stop breathing for a few seconds. I cover my goose pimples with soap and look out the narrow bathroom skylight.

I remember quickening the pace, sliding in mud until I caught the shadow running ahead. It was all about the chase. I remember shadow-man stopping and stepping aside in the wood and, like a true gentleman, ushering me through, "after you Sir" he said. "Sir!" How funny. I found momentum in that final mile, as the sea exploded on rocks immediately below, froth-fragments forced into the air like fireworks. I leaned, pushed, stretched my stride. I remember now, I remember: Picking my way down 200, maybe 300 wooden steps smeared in mud but not caring. The descent beckoned. Just keep moving, seeking the sanctuary of Oxwich Bay where white flags surrendered to the wind and chaotic footprint patterns indicated all those who had gone before. Yes, I remember: Oxwich Bay had been struck by two rock falls at the start of the year, the largest rockfalls in the UK in recent years. Boulders the size of houses came away from the limestone cliffs near to where we gathered at the start. We stood amid the collapse.

And I remember the wet sting on skin. The foretaste of winter.

I walk downstairs backwards for breakfast because it is less painful on the knees and sit alone, opposite a huge dining room mirror, which makes the room appear limitless. Chair legs scrape across the floor. A newspaper, folded in half, rests on the table with the words "THE NATION REMEMBERS" parading along its crease with a photograph of the Queen wearing a poppy. The waitress bangs a teapot on to the table, tea spitting across the table cloth. I remember where I am.

Something is uncomfortable. I pull three pebbles from my trouser pocket and rest them on the table. One white, one granite-grey, one peach-coloured. Where did these come from? I peer at the map of yesterday's race on my phone, expanding and shrinking the map with thumb and finger to locate the precise place. It was somewhere near...near to Horton. Yes. We had come through the saltmarshes. It was Port-Eynon Bay, just before the last checkpoint at 23 miles where I skirted the tidal edge as it advanced, then retreated, churning pebbles in its wake. I collected dozens, each pebble unique upon inspection. The pebbles became ballast to keep me anchored to the earth as the wind pummelled and pushed. Then I let them all go, saving these three. A double rainbow appeared in the bay as the rain eased and the horizon lit up a fierce silver, as if sea and sky were soldered together, everything becoming seamless.

The dining room is now empty except for a family of four in the corner. A toddler litters the floor with baked beans and there is a black sausage steaming beneath his high chair. At least I hope it is a sausage. I lift my teacup and stare into the mirror.

I remember: Standing in the race marquee collecting my race number just before dawn, the sound of rain on the tent canvas was like gravel dropping from a great height. The faces of 150 runners, each shrouded in a hood pulled tight ensuring their heads didn't detach from their shoulders. White race flags convulsing along the beach and the words "NEVER GIVE UP" on the inflatable start line.

And the wet sting on skin.

The race began with needing to avoid a huge dead tree stump that looked like the severed head of a Triceratops. The course followed the Gower Way, continuing through Nicholston Burrows, through dying bracken, before arriving at Gower's highest point, Cefn Bryn (meaning the 'spine of the hill') from where both sides of the peninsula were visible. I look at the phone map for reference. We ran past Arthur's Stone, a 25 foot boulder perched on the common, covering a neolithic burial chamber. Legend says King Arthur removed a stone from his shoe whilst travelling through Carmenthenshire and threw it across the Loughor Estuary. By the time the stone came to rest, it had increased in size to a boulder. The stone left as a child but arrived as a fully fledged Rock. I swipe the screen-map to the left, events becoming alive to my mind again. Through Hillend at checkpoint one and onto Ryer's Down when the sun broke through cloud. Climbing to Stormy Castle just south of Llanmadoc before connecting with the Wales Coast Path. On the map, one named place leads to another named place leads to another, but out there on the run the Names didn't matter. It was just the process, the whole damned hard thing, where all the unnamed in-betweenness was one continuous movement. And the stinging skin, a reminder of being alive.

The rule, my one rule. I remembered. *It doesn't matter how long it takes, just keep going.*

The tide at Llangennith was out, leaving litter and seaweed spewed along the beach. I ran through the sand dunes, picked my way down Spaniard Rocks, found a soft landing onto the beach where hundreds of scuffed trainer marks dodged dead jellyfish. Black seaweed and foil crisp packets lay entwined in mutual defeat.

I remember: It broke my heart. There was the lid to an oil can, bottle caps, slim pen lids, plastic shrapnel everywhere. A fluorescent cigarette lighter lay next to an air freshener spray can, its nozzle half-buried in the sand, as if in denial. A chocolate bar wrapper, red print faded to yellow. One, two, three, four... too many large plastic bottles to count, all dented. A ping pong ball bandaged in seaweed. A sandwich box, empty of munitions. A rear car lamp with wires like antennae. I took photographs. It was a crime scene.

Then it began.

Gathering all the broken parts in my arms, stuffing what I could into my coat pockets. Another runner overtook me. "Nice work" he said. "I could do with a bag really" I replied. He slowed, then turned toward me. From his jacket sleeve he conjured a white dustbin liner which went flick-flick-flick in the wind. Into the bag the beach litter poured, like rockfall. It was a mile to the next checkpoint and the quantity of litter huddled and held between us became overwhelming. I stopped running to watch a hundred wading birds pecking at the tideline, inspecting their territory, cluttered with the rubbish we humans intended for the sea. At my feet were clams the size of a child's hand. Clams have a heart, a basic cardiovascular structure with arteries and veins, a living, breathing thing. These were swathed in a black dustbin liner so the clams looked like they were in an unzipped body bag. Its two equal parts, hinged together, open like a butterfly, revealing unexpected symmetry.

I remember:

Standing on the beach.

A human silhouette, arms full of discarded and damaged things. A body became the landscape.

It wept.

Memories from yesterday flicker like a slideshow, details edited, the pernicious mind selecting, filtering, sorting, archiving. Remembering is an act of re-creation and the past becomes new and different as a result. Pieces get moved around. The story never quite stays the same.

I remember: There were coves and caves, places around the headland where smugglers once hid. At one point I saw a runner strip off, the shock of his white chest reflecting in the low sun. It must have been where I left the litter at the checkpoint. Across the grey plate of sea the limestone silhouette of Worm's Head arose from the waves, its back and head above water, looking toward the horizon. I felt the chill-wind of a thousand years blowing like Norse echoes. And the wet sting on skin. Winter biting.

Swiping through yesterday's photos I come across one of a stone pillar we ran past whose lower half is adorned in red paint, with two words painted white: Cofiwch Drywerin, meaning "Remember Tryweryn". In the 1960s Liverpool City Council decided to flood the Tryweryn Valley to create a reservoir but didn't tell the Welsh authorities about the decision or those who lived there. Despite protests in parliament, English authorities flooded the Welsh valley and communities hundreds of years old, like Capel Celyn, were lost. The Remembering was a small thing to begin with, just two words painted by a journalist on some old cottage wall to get people to remember what happened. But the words became a symbol, then a contest, when the slogan was defaced with swastikas, before being repainted. It was vandalised again when someone painted "Forget Tryweryn" in Welsh, before being repaired once more. A relentless cycle of remembering and erasing memory. As if the crumbling cottage wall couldn't bear the words any longer, the message of remembering was blown like dandelion seed across the Welsh landscape. The slogan now appears in dozens of places, including yesterday's race route. Next to the original crumbling wall, a new wall was built and the words Fe Godwn Ni Eto painted on it, meaning "We'll rise again". The message was even on a banner at the London marathon this year.

Somewhere along the cliff edge an old dream returned to mind, from when life felt upside-down. In the dream was a man sat in a chair, quiet and still. He opened his eyes, as if waking up, and spoke just one word to me: "Sessonance", he said. That was the dream. Upon waking I checked whether "sessonance" existed as a word. Apart from a man born in 1891 who had Sessonance as his middle name, it wasn't in any dictionary. I guess the origins of this invented dream-word probably include *sessilis* from the Latin "to sit", *sonare* meaning "the sound of", plus *caesura*, which in music indicates a rest. "Sessonance": to experience an internal resonance with where you are; the fusion of your senses with stillness, silence and your surroundings.

A dream, shaken to the surface by movement and the stinging rain. Stillness rising.

Breakfast arrives. I cut through a sausage and the knife clanks hard on to the plate. The family of four look my way, signalling that I need to quieten down. Then the father in the corner slaps both hands on his table and stands, ready to battle with his baked bean-tossing child. In the reflection of the mirror he appears to have no legs.

I remember: We climbed onto Rhossili Down running among cairns, hundreds of mounds and humps. Every step forced you to look down. Runners higher up appeared as shadows, bent over as they climbed, hands clasped on knees. Halfway up the climb, I turned to see how far we had come and a lady behind me spoke. I saw her mouth move but the wind stole her words. I waited until she was by my side. "Brutal. I said it's brutal", she shouted into my ear. "Yes, but…" and I pointed to the scene behind her: the long beachbreak, the land kissed yellow and shining from the morning storm, the sea stretching forever like whale-skin, and eternity hovering above the horizon, rising to nothingness. She put her hand to her mouth as if eating the awe.

I remember: Sheep stood on the cliff edge oblivious to the possibility of falling. The coastal path turned away from Worm's Head and descended. A narrow path next to an old stone wall had become a sloppy mudslide. The harder I tried to stand upright, the more I fell, erecting myself like a trig point from which to get my own bearings but slipping again. Control was no use, you had to trust instinct, trust your feet, trust the gravity beyond your body. A steep slope appeared ahead. Despite the fear, I abandoned myself to the descent, spiralling like a puppy chasing its tail, waving my arms. Walkers passing in the opposite direction eyed this maniacal dance with suspicion as I careered, zig-zagging left to right, backpack jostling, before doing star-jumps as I reached the plateau. My body peaked in the air like an inverted exclamation mark, an **i** suspended in space, the tiny dot of the mind temporarily detached from the body, before returning to earth.

As I remember, a smile arcs across my face like a Geminid meteor.

I stare into the white light of the dining room window, unaware the waitress has refilled the tea pot at some point.

In the telling and remembering of the story, I feel as if I am shaking something out of myself, an expired past perhaps. Coding it in words creates distance between Me and It. I am no longer trapped in a story seeking escape, but have become the story-teller. The one who shapes it, cohering new meanings, conjuring new hope. By telling the story, however fragmented it sounds and however fragile it feels, it becomes possible to recover those parts which have been excluded. Dots join, broken edges soften.

We remember who we are as we make peace with the past. Knife and fork rest parallel on the plate.

It's true. You do rise again.

I ease myself up from the chair and struggle up the stairs to collect my things. As I pull the hotel room key from my pocket, a pebble from Port-Eynon Bay spills out and plonks down the stairs, rolling until it reaches the bottom, yielding to the gravity of its fall.

I remember: One final red dot loiters on the map at home, like an escapee, hiding in the Northumberland outback. I am coming to meet you.

WINTER

"Reaching our limit is like finding a doorway to sanity"
—Pema Chödrön

Bright blood pools in my hand as I withdraw it from my head. The car boot hadn't opened fully, and with my attention distracted by a ghost-white cat sat on a roof, the night behind it like a cloak, my head collided with something metallic and sharp. I staggered and fell. My neighbour heard a yell and sprinted down the staircase. I felt his hand on my shoulder. "You alright mate? D'ya fancy an ambulance?" he asked, as if offering me a cup of tea. In the end the wound only needed glueing together but in the ambulance I met Mel and Kim. Two paramedics, not the 1980s pop music duo.

Mel drives and makes the blue lights spin whilst Kim wipes rivulets of blood from my forehead, then slowly from around each eye. "Christopher" she says, "stop hyper-ventilating. You sound like you're running the last mile of the London marathon". I mention, between gasps, I have run it twice. Kim began running earlier this year by using the popular "Couch to 5k" programme when she couldn't ride her horses. "I never thought I'd get into running but it gives me the chance to box things off, sort my head out. I'm slow but I'm good getting up the hills." Her hand passes across my face, wiping blood from the bridge of my nose. Mel calls from the driver seat that she's a marathon runner too and tells me about ultra races I have never heard of, like the 180 mile-long Dragon Back race in Wales. My hyper-ventilating worsens. "Nothing wrong with a 5k" Kim reassures me, then explains how their work impacts them. "To be fair, it's not the physical health stuff so much, it's the mental health. Last week we recovered a 55 year old man who hung himself in front of his neighbour. Yesterday it was a man in his twenties. That was bad. The suicide rate here is sky-rocketing." Kim pulls a blanket over my legs. "How did we get into this?" she says, as-if to herself, "this idea that everything has to be perfect. Perfect job, perfect partner, perfect kids, perfect home" spitting out the p of each perfection. "It's shit."

"What's your work?" Mel yells from the driver seat above the roar of the ambulance engine. I tell them about working as a coach in schools, and that I'm writing a book about running in nature and recovery from "stuff". "You have to keep going, you hear me?" urges Kim, leaning down as if to kiss me, "and tell people we have to talk about how it really is. We have to talk about how we really are."

Back home, the top left corner of the map sags away from the wall. There is a solitary dot remaining, a long way from home. It will be a final confrontation with the darkness.

KIELDER WATER

You can't go back the way you came

Darkness creeps up from the forest floor. Rain, the forerunner to Storm Atiyah arriving from Ireland, has fingered its way into the rucksack, raincoat, socks. This final run, final month, final mile and I am lost. More than that, I feel scared. At the crook of Bull Crag Peninsula, with 20-something miles in my legs, I left the path which tracked the lake perimeter. I don't know why, perhaps I thought it would be clever or interesting to explore. A scuffed rut weaves through felled Scots pines then narrows until there is no path. I turn, but in the forest-shadows at dusk there is no trace of where I came from or where I should go next. I turn, and turn, but darkness has come. I check supplies: two empty water bottles, a foil blanket, a bruised apple. There is no phone signal and the phone battery icon is reduced to a blood-red rectangle showing 9% power remaining. Freya's Cabin, an open-ended wooden hut stationed at the reservoir edge could provide shelter but that was almost an hour of running ago, and I can't determine in which direction to run. My gut says "you can't go back the way you came".

I need a satellite image to illuminate my place in things, or the Navigator's Triangle to appear in the sky declaring "You Are HERE", but the sky is dense cloud. There's no help from above. In the absence of a map, phone signal, stars, signposts, human or divine help, I follow instinct and just run, dwarfed by hundreds of pines erect as javelins. Storm history is everywhere. Shards of forest turf twelve feet high tilt perpendicular to the forest floor like earthen gravestones and in the dim-dusk I dodge them as best as I can but inevitably shoulder barge one and find it immovable. Time evaporates in this liminal space. *Where am I?* I can feel them rising, the old anxieties, the twisted stomach feeling, the memory of that dark presence in the room at night. For a few seconds the phone flickers with a 4G signal and a text message arrives from Max, a friend I haven't spoken with for a year: "Hey, I'm listening to the new Ride album, 'This is not a safe place' and I thought of you. Hope all is well?" The text arrives twice, as if for emphasis. Then the phone signal vanishes. I wave the phone around like a flare but there's no connection. The text echoes in my head, "This is not a safe place, this is not a safe place, this is not..." as the forest wraps winter darkness around me. Fear is not a feeling, it is a taste in my mouth.

In its two-dimensional form on a map Kielder Water looks like flames thrown from a dragon's mouth. It is the largest artificial lake in the UK by capacity of water, created when Kielder dam was constructed in 1979, and surrounded by one of the largest human-made forests in Europe, a mix of deciduous and pine, with wetland, woodland and grassland habitats. Little more than a 100 years earlier coal was extracted from the valley, the railway lines which transported it now submerged beneath the water, along with the railway station, mines, quarries, coke ovens, lime kilns and farms. All just the wet bones of history. Swimming in the reservoir are trout, minnow, eels and stone loach. Otters hunt along the shoreline and common frogs and palmate newts spawn in its shallow edges. Gliding across it you can see pochards, tufted ducks, teal and goldeneye. But not today. Mid-morning, mid-December, as I set off running alone from Kielder dam car park, a solitary goose swims as if it has arrived too early for something, or too late.

I first ran around Kielder Water five years ago, in the official

Kielder Water marathon event organised by British athletic legend Steve Cram, winner of the 800 metres at the 1984 Los Angeles Olympics. Cram ran circuits of this reservoir for his training, then 30 years later realised its circumference was nearly a marathon distance and decided to create the official Kielder race in 2010. The following year, a runner claimed third place by catching the bus, cutting six miles off the distance. Crossing the dam bridge I feel determined to complete the whole circuit, anti-clockwise, sticking to the lakeside path and resisting use of public transport. No need for a detailed map. Simple.

Over the bridge a small cruise boat, "Osprey", rests upon a trolley, inconspicuous at the shore edge. Kielder is one of the most southerly places in the UK where ospreys are seen between March and late summer, usually in the early morning light, dropping from heights of 220 feet, their wings whipped back, talons thrust forward to seize a perch, trout or pike. They were absent from Kielder for around 200 years but in the last decade their number has grown to six breeding pairs. Ospreys migrate alone, following their own 3,000 mile odyssey to Africa.

I ascend a muddy bank and run through a slim avenue of pines causing the lake to appear locked behind prison bars. Following the Lakeside Way is straight forward, and at the Belling peninsula, one of many architectural structures around the lake comes into view. The Wave Chamber, a beehive-shaped stone construction is made from over 80 tons of local stone, enough to fill ten double-decker buses. Cracking the door latch down, I feel a sharp chill on my fingertips and step inside, hesitating in the near-dark before shutting the door. It creaks behind me like an exaggerated sound effect. It is a cold, blind space. A white-washed circle of stone becomes visible upon the floor, gleaming like a dull eye. In the chamber a mirror and lens project an image of waves onto the floor. This is the theory, anyway. All I see is a dirty white blur beneath my trainers, but the construct amplifies the sound of water so I feel an oscillation between the solidity of the stone-stacked cone and the fluidity of water lapping beneath. I close my eyes and imagine walking on water. Words return to mind from years ago, when I stood by the River Avon near home, my heart unsteadied from the ending of married life. I watched the swell of the high river, wondering from where the river originated and to where it flowed. Ripped branches protruded and chewed-up litter attempted to cling to something solid. Quiet words flowed to me from somewhere: "Things are always changing", words that brought an unexpected wave of peacefulness amid the mental turbulence at that time.

Now, here I am alone in a dank-dark stone beehive, between lake-edge and winter-forest. The miracle I realise now is not to walk on water but just to Be Here in the first place. The door latch yields under my thumb. A crack, a squeak. I step back into veiled forest light and run across a mattress of pine needles, wood-scent rising as my toes crush and caress what has fallen. I continue west past Belvedere from where the summertime ferry operates. Step upon step, mile upon mile, memory upon memory, like a tree expanding with new rings, a story leafed with new pages.

Turning a corner there's an empty open-ended wooden hut raised off the ground, a natural pausing place after running five miles. Robin's Hut, situated on the remote north shoreline is a cedar shingle hut, its simplicity in deliberate contrast to the intricacy of Freya's Cabin on the opposite side of the lake. The pair of shelters, according to the architects, are an exploration of weaving together wood with words, story with landscape. Robin's Hut represents the island-loving man who builds himself a simple shelter in the woods, two walls, a roof, and a floor to sit upon. A perfect place for reading Thoreau. The architects imagined story is that Robin built a boat which Freya believed was for rowing across the lake to her cabin on the south bank, but with the sun in Robin's eyes, he couldn't see her cabin and set off on his own adventure, osprey-like, a solo migration across the waters. Realising Robin was moving away rather than towards her, Freya cried tears of gold which she wrapped around her cabin, shown in the skilled flowing wood lattice. But then from a distance, her cabin of tears glinted, catching Robin's eye. Out of curiosity he reoriented his boat, arriving at her cabin. Upon finding Freya and talking together about flowers and trees, Robin invited her to join him on "his adventure". I didn't realise talking about flowers could be so seductive. I sit on Robin's muddy floorboards for a few minutes, eating a banana, looking across the waters through the mist, from this wooden structure toward the other. I imagine the other sits empty. I wonder if Freya will have a say in the direction they travel or is she just there for the ride. Freya could certainly teach Robin a thing or two about carpentry.

This rain wasn't forecast until late afternoon. As the lakeside path turns north then north-west, drizzle saturates my beard, causing arm hairs to appear emboldened. Beneath Pithouse Crags jugular machinery for harvesting trees lays dormant. Then a yell. "WAY SHOUT!" A man on a mountain bike spurts past, the complex mechanics of his bike clattering as he pulls it left and right, weaving around logs with speed and skill, the metallic noise a contrast to the shruh-shruh of my feet shuffling over the shroud of the forest floor. As he fades from view I translate his yell as "Watch out" and my mind returns to my uncle, tartan blanket across his knees in an NHS wheelchair in the Brighton marathon, sounding the air horn. I arrive where the path dissects the old Plashetts railway line whose tracks lead into the water as if pulled into the underworld, submerged into

====== wherevernext====== wherevernext=====

They look alien. Four enormous cubes, each six foot high, emerging from the mist looking like shrink-wrapped shipping containers plonked here by mistake. The "Salmon Cubes" are a set of sculptures representing the salmon's life cycle, initiated by The Environment Agency to promote awareness of the salmon population in the River Tyne. Originally, a shoal of ten cubes were positioned along the River Tyne's banks following the migration of salmon from Kielder Water to the Tyne river-mouth, then out to sea. The six foot high mirrored ridges of the first cube cause my body to appear split into four sections. Named "Reflection", the mirror-box is inspired by the myths and legends of salmon. Leaning against the cube, I remember looking down the waters of the River Tummel in Pitlochry after the first marathon in Kinloch Rannoch, hoping to see salmon leap up the HHHHHHH ladder, from lower to higher. Their name comes from the Latin *salire*, meaning "to leap" (and links to the word "resilience"), sometimes becoming injured in the process when their silver-skinned bodies slap against concrete and metal obstacles. A risk-taking fish, obeying an instinct to come home.

The second cube, "Birth", is an overlay of red and white plastic with different size holes, representing the pea-sized eggs salmon lay in gravel beds. Pine saplings and brambles poke through from inside the cube. Each side of the third cube, "Scales", is adorned with sixteen rows and sixteen columns of semi-bent mirror discs, more than a thousand in total, representing the agility of the salmon's armour. I lean in until my breath mists the mirror. The final cube, "Colours", is a series of white, grey and orange oblong flaps which you can spin to change the colour, inspired by the changing colours of the salmon throughout their life cycle.

It is midday and the view across the reservoir shrinks as the temperature falls and the mist lowers. Diverting from the main path, I investigate the Janus chairs, another architectural feature along the shoreline: a set of three huge but differently sized chairs, like something from Goldilocks and the Three Bears. Their different forms are based on the idea of flower petals in various stages of unfolding. Each chair can be rotated, I discover with considerable effort, to face each other as if to invite conversation, or turn outward to the water in contemplation. Each chair is constructed by laminating together multiple small pieces of thin wood-strips which provide a versatility that old wood doesn't have. Each chair is backed with stainless steel to reflect the surroundings.

Turning the three chairs to face one another, I climb onto the smallest chair, about three times the width of a typical dining chair, then balance on its edge to stare across the water. Janus, the Roman god after which the chairs are named (and from whom the month January is named), has quite a job description: Janus is the god of gates, bridges, passageways, archways and doorways, as well as the god of time, beginnings and endings. He is usually depicted as having two faces, one facing the past, the other towards the future. In the 21st century we would probably add to his task list so it includes subways, kissing gates, elevators and train station turnstiles. Although Janus would probably see all that coming. But he is not the god of maps, because Atlas has that territory covered. Janus is a multi-functional, transient god, rotating 360 degrees like the chair upon which I stand. I like him. He is useful if you need to find your way.

Rain runs in dashed lines off the steel spine of the chair. Can looking back help us look forward? I reflect on today being the final marathon and remember the first dot, running around Loch Rannoch, Number 1234 pinned to my front representing a beginning. Then finding silence beneath stars and Geminid meteors. Running up-and-back along a disused railway line like childhood messages stuck on repeat. Then I fell face first in Fearfall Woods. Are these just random dots on a map? Does anything join them? Running across a barren fen during Storm Freya and collapsing in the Abbey, before returning to face the failure when the land was lit yellow. Running head-down along the crumbling Jurassic coastline then beneath the towering Pinnacles of Cheddar Gorge at moonrise. Weaving through the Mourne mountain foothills over copper streams and not squashing the frog. Dot, dot, dot, dot. Conquering a Welsh mountain peak before it then conquered me. Getting lost in a forest looking for a wayward donkey. The Tors of Dartmoor, the single fly agaric mushroom and so many lost men. Does the body remember each strike, each sight, each step? I remember the two coastlines, Beachy Head where the wind thrust me up the final hill of the Seven Sisters, and Gower peninsula where I abandoned myself on the descents. Perhaps this journey has just been a chance to give the mind and body a bloody good shake up. Perching on the lip of the Janus chair, I remember Lucas escaping from Shetland, the blonde-plaited, ultra running single mum, and the graphic designer running again after being attacked. What keeps them going? Is the search for recovery irrepressible in us all? I leap from the child-chair to the middle-sized chair which budges beneath my weight, before stepping up onto the largest of the chairs. I ease my shoulders back, raise my chin, centring myself upon its edge and gaze across the waters.

The choice to run within all these landscapes has helped with a mental migration from living in the past towards noticing what is present. I am just a speck in a magnificent swirling universe. Landing in the now - feet striking the earth again...again...again, over half a million times since the run in Loch Rannoch - has lessened *prapanca*, or at least helped me notice the breeding thoughts a little sooner. The Present has shifted from background to foreground.

A year from now my friend Max will text me again, this time reminding me, out of the blue, that 20 years ago I donated nearly half my vinyl record collection to him to keep. I have no recollection of this. After a year of messaging to-and-fro, because understandably Max is quite attached to the gift, the day comes when I drive two hours to his home and am reunited with over 200 vinyl albums, 12" and 7" singles from my teenage years. Records associated with people, places and passions I thought were gone from my memory forever. Kneeling on the carpet in his lounge I hold a 7" single, "The Living Years", showing an hourglass with sand flowing from the past back to the present. I flip it over, and over, and laugh.

Standing on the edge of the largest Janus chair, I breathe out. Survive, Return...Restore.

I have often escaped into my own headspace for refuge, but climbing inside another head is a different experience. This head is a two-storey timber construction, made from over 3000 pieces of European larch, held together without nails or bolts and finished with chainsaw and grinder giving it the feel of imperfection. The ears are formed as trumpets reaching into the head's interior so you can enter the mouth, climb the stairs and look out through its eyes and listen to the forest from within. The head is called Silvas Capitalis, a play on the Latin for "forest head". The open-mouthed head sits in the Kielder woodland looking toward the reservoir. The American artists conceived the structure as "a watcher, an imagined presence who has observed the landscape over the past millennia", inspired by the gods of Celtic folklore, represented by a head without a body.

Approaching the mouth, I reach the dark space of the doorway but stop as three pairs of boots shuffle in a narrow patch of light at the entrance. A conversation reverberates on the inside of the head, musical male voices, like a cello and two bass. "What does Sally think?" asks one. "How should I know, she's a woman" another jokes, "I can get inside this head but I sure canna get inside hers". They laugh. "Would ya want anyone gettin' inside ya head?" the third voice asks, and there is a pause, before the cello-like voice speaks. "I've felt locked inside mine me whole life. Just wish someone coulda show me the bloody way out". Pairs of feet scuff the earth and a metal flask gets knocked over and clinks on the cold ground. I climb up the stairs and look out through its eyes. What was it Thoreau said? Something about the miracle of looking, even for a moment, through the eyes of the other. To do this requires a willingness to see different things and to see things differently.

The wind accelerates and rain permeates my jacket fabric. For the next three miles I keep to the path like an obedient child, passing Gowanburn where the reservoir narrows, then over the Kielder viaduct to Butteryhaugh where the reservoir is at its closest point to Scotland. Mist absorbs everything. I have been running (and getting distracted by sculptures) for over three hours and am not yet halfway. The car is parked 14 miles away. The sun, not that it has showed up today, sets at 3.40 p.m. Less than two hours of bleak-light remain. I should have started the process earlier. I should have brought a phone power pack. I should have brought torchlight. I should have noted the telephone number of The Hollybush Inn at Greenhaugh. My head swarms with my mistakes, and I start to worry. When I worry I ruminate, thoughts breeding at speed. The past comes back like a flood and within minutes I am rehearsing all the wounds of the last few years. "Stop!" I say out loud, "just stop!", an audible way of catching myself in the act before retreating into the past.

Kielder Waterside Park. When I was last here pockets of spectators stood in anoraks handing out isotonic drinks in plastic cups, and the marquee by the finish line blared out "A Sky Full Of Stars" by Coldplay. Today there are no crowds, applause, flags or plastic cups. But there is music: "Snow is falling, all around us, everybody's having fun". The sound system proclaims this lie from speakers hidden half way up pine trees, with pathetic strings of fairy lights creating, apparently, an enchanted forest. Enchanted: where anything can happen. I pass a plastic toadstool, eight feet high, swamped in Christmas decorations. A red squirrel scampers up a tree nearby, unimpressed. An hour before sunset, seven miles to run. Stay on the path. Nothing clever now Christopher, you've got this.

No phone signal, no map, no help. Just darkness and the crick-crack of the forest at dusk. I close my eyes and listen. There is the faint sound of a vehicle from somewhere. I move in its direction. Stop, listen, adjust. After a while a red light flashes through columns of pine trees. I find the empty C-road, rain shining on its surface. Ten minutes, nothing. Twenty minutes, nothing. I stand and trust that help will come.

A motorhome approaches, the registration plate boldly declaring USA 222. This is a guy who knows who he is. I wave my arms, two fluorescent sticks swaying in the rain. It is a left-hand drive vehicle. The window lowers, and I utter the words I have found hard to say my whole life, "I am lost. I need help". Emotion rises to my lips. "I've been running for nearly six hours and…" The man narrows his eyes, sussing me out. "I'm just really tired and I don't know where I am." The driver stares, tight lipped as I try not to let anxiety get the better of me. He calculates. I expect his motorhome is clean and dry. Do I pose a risk? His wife leans over. She investigates a map on her phone until we agree on where we think we are. "Okay, get the fook in mate" the driver says. I fondle various handles hanging off his van. "Mate. Door's round other fookin side".

The driver tells me about their shopping trip that afternoon in Newcastle. "We didn't plan on driving out here did we babe, just followed an urge." I shiver on their back seat, rain pooling at my feet and mixing with the mud from my trail shoes which streams across the clean floor of their motorhome. "Maybe we were meant to help you" his wife says. Headlights pierce the mist. "Here!" I shout. He swings his van into a car park as I roll across the seat. I get out and express my thanks. But my car isn't in the car park. It's definitely not there because it is the wrong car park. It is difficult to tell them apart in the dark. "Wait!" I shout, and the brake lights of the motorhome light up. "Fookin' hell mate you gives us a heart attack" he says, his elbow resting on the open window. In the next car park a mile down the road his headlights illuminate my car. I stand in the dark and wave them goodbye.

Leaning against the car I check the distance run today: 25.6 miles. I failed to complete the circuit of Kielder Water. I remember my self-imposed rules, all one of them.

Rule No. 1: It doesn't matter how long the process takes, just keep going.

There is no way I am shortchanging on the deal I made with myself. Going the distance is the task. I shuffle across the top of Kielder dam bridge, then back again. Then back across the bridge, as if reconciling the last solitary dot on the map with the whole. An icy breeze kisses my lips. Puddles splash, disturbed by feet which barely leave the ground.

It is done: 26.2 miles. Fourteen trail marathons from one winter to the next. The phone battery says 3%. I feel a strange rejuvenation as if dopamine in the brain is giving high-fives to all the frazzled neurons it has left in its wake. Relief.

In the car I celebrate by ripping open a packet of chicken noodle soup and pouring it into a flask of lukewarm water. It tastes like punishment but I am thankful for the warmth. Thankful for the chair. Thankful for help. Thankful for each breath which mists the car windscreen. I turn the radio on and recognise the tune. Ah, what is it? It's that film soundtrack, it's "Superman".

I remember: A photograph clings to the fridge door at home. A child with a cape, pants over leggings and a paper 'S' pinned to his chest. I laugh hard, spewing half-eaten noodles onto my lap. It's all you can do when you come back to yourself, because where did you go all this time?

Part III
A GEOGRAPHY OF HOPE

In the Roman calendar, today is a new year festival in honour of Anna Perenna, Roman goddess of renewal and the returning year. The festival involved sacrificing a criminal or elderly man in a ritual intended to purify society. Today, a dull mid-March day, is also my birthday, but no more sacrifice is required. I am recovering from the Portland marathon a few weeks ago, enduring another coastline, a race where I paused at the halfway point and a marshal called Boris strapped up my twisted ankle. I finished the race but resolved that my body needed a rest. In one week's time the country will go into its first lockdown due to the coronavirus pandemic. Life will fall apart again for a while. My business survives the pandemic with help from my dad. Like many others, I experience Long Covid and won't run for a year due to chronic fatigue, the legacy being a tremor in my right hand. Soon after the pandemic I join other volunteers in planting native broadleaf trees in Binton, an acorn's throw from where I ran the night of the Geminid meteors. And then life will slowly come together. Work flourishes. I will be asked to write a book on grief with my partner, Jess, and I join an athletics club, not to win races but to make friends. Anglesey and Inverness marathons become dots turning red to blue.

But today, who knows all the good and challenging things yet to unfold? As a birthday present to myself I fetch a couple of black dustbin bags and custard-coloured rubber gloves and walk to Dorothy's

Wood, my geography of hope, in search of an exchange. The woodland works upon me more than I work upon it. Each tiny act - picking up a discarded crisp packet, retrieving a crushed drinks can from tangled undergrowth - is multiplied back as reward in the form of blackthorn blossom-scent and symphonic birdsong. A jay flashes through the branches, a buzzard circles above, seeking.

The woodland, this place of complexity, full of hidden resource, has become a sanctuary, a safe place where listening becomes possible again. A place to notice the presence of recovery: feeling safer in the body; attending to the present moment more often; less self-criticism; knowing the signs of old worries coming to the surface then resetting after a difficulty; self-compassion now breeding compassion towards others; relationships are in better balance and the old drives have softened. This is sanity: Where everything comes to a point of gentle stillness, where everything belongs. All that is gone, all that is here and the tentative future unfolding from *today*. I feel both anchored and animated here. *Sessonance*. A fusion of inner and outer quietude.

As we move through nature, nature moves through us, seeping in, dismantling, reconfiguring us, until we become permeable to the flow of life. Something deeper, truer, more whole comes through. But recovery is not a destination. Our true work in the world has only just begun. Blackbirds sing. I look up and around. Everything is changing.

ACKNOWLEDGEMENTS

Thank you to Phil & Carol Williams for your kindness and a safe house. To Dr. Rosa Chillari, Murray Scholefield, Mark Foster, John Hill, Katherine Long, Mark Humphries, Tim Robson, John Whittington, Jamie Pennington, Jo & Darren Turner, John D, Linda Y, Max Hayek and Jeanie Davies for timely help in different ways. To the many writers whose own words guided, especially Rob MacFarlane for encouraging me to write and for the inspiration of "The Wild Places". To all the runners, event organisers, helpers and dormitory companions along the way. To Shantigosha, my meditation teacher. To Claire Marr and Debbie Chapman for encouragement to publish this story and Benita Thompson for stunning cover design. To Auntie Sandra & family for generous support over the years, and Uncle Andrew - a true hero. To my dad, Elizabeth, Mark and Helen for grace, meals & sofa beds. To my mum, you're still with me. To my children K, MJ & T for being who you are and to Hannah for your dedication to our children. To Jess for your boundless love and humour.

ABOUT THE AUTHOR

Christopher Spriggs is a dad to three children, and founder of both Lifespace Trust, a mentoring charity for young people, and Heads Up Now Ltd., which coaches leaders, teams and organisations through transition. He enjoys listening to vinyl records and walking the coast.

You can find him on LinkedIn.

| W: lifespace.org.uk | W: headsupnow.uk |
| YouTube @RunningOffTheMap |

By the same author

"*The Reason I Run: How Two Men Transformed Tragedy into the Greatest Race of their Lives*", published by Summersdale, June 2015

"*Grief, Loss and How to Cope: A Self-Help Guide for Difficult Times*", co-authored with Jess Smallwood, published by Summersdale, July 2022

"*Grief: A Guided Workbook to Help You Heal*" published by Summersdale, May 2024

RESOURCES

- British Association for Counselling and Psychotherapy (BACP) is the professional association for members of the counselling profession in the UK: www.BACP.co.uk
- Campaign Against Living Miserably (CALM) exists to prevent people taking their own life. They provide a free 5pm to midnight helpline 365 days of the year: 0800 58 58 58
- Mental Health First Aid (MHFA) offers expert guidance and training to support mental health in the workplace and beyond: www.mhfaengland.org
- Life Love Leadership, founded by John Whittington, offers systemic workshops which illuminate the complex dynamics, repeating patterns and hidden resources in life, intimate relationships and work: www.LifeLoveLeadership.com

Printed in Great Britain
by Amazon